MW00809924

# SAVVY ESTATE PLANNING

2ND EDITION *WITH NEW IRA LAWS*

# SAVVY ESTATE PLANNING

## WHAT YOU NEED TO KNOW BEFORE YOU TALK TO THE RIGHT LAWYER

## JAMES L. CUNNINGHAM, JR.

**LIONCREST**
PUBLISHING

SAVVY ESTATE PLANNING
*What You Need to Know Before You Talk to the Right Lawyer*

SECOND EDITION

ISBN   978-1-5445-2789-5   *Hardcover*
       978-1-5445-2790-1   *Paperback*
       978-1-5445-2791-8   *Ebook*
       978-1-5445-2792-5   *Audiobook*

# CONTENTS

———

# FOREWORD

BY LONNIE MARTIN, CHAIR,
VISTAGE INTERNATIONAL/
SACRAMENTO

---

If you're like me, you don't spend a lot of time contemplating your own death or its implications for others. We find it much more cheerful to assume that unhappy events will occur in some faraway future—a future we don't need to consider anytime soon. Like Scarlett O'Hara in *Gone with the Wind,* most of us say, "I'll think about it tomorrow."

The result? People often leave a costly mess for their loved ones. Too often, much of what they worked for in this life also ends up gone with the wind—gone to taxes, probate lawyers, and undeserving predators.

Jim Cunningham is trying to wake us all up and force us to think about the future, as if that future really is coming *tomorrow,* and we have to prepare for it *today.*

Just as importantly, he's trying to cut through the jargon and make a complicated subject both readable and understandable. With this short book, he hopes to stop us all from making the big mistakes he sees people make every day.

I've come to know Jim because he joined one of my Vistage CEO peer groups, and I've been helping as a coach for the business end of his stellar legal practice. As a result, it's been easy for me to see the passion he has for this kind of work—a passion I've seen grow stronger year after year.

Jim followed his dad into the profession of helping people prepare for their possible future incapacity, their ultimate demise, and above all, their legacy. He started CunninghamLegal to focus exclusively on estate law, and he's one of the few lawyers certified specifically for estate planning and probate law.

Over the years, Jim has taught me more than I ever thought I'd know about trusts, wills, and inheritance. Above all, I've learned how few adults realize the way estate laws affect them, both before and after their deaths.

People don't understand the issues or the terminology, and

for sure, they don't understand the myriad of state and federal laws. And honestly, why would anybody want to master this arcane body of knowledge, if it weren't their full-time job?

This book doesn't try to make you into an estate lawyer, and especially not a do-it-yourself estate planner. Instead, it offers you insider savvy about the issues, pitfalls, and real opportunities within estate law.

You'll learn about the often-missed ways you can help yourself and your heirs during your lifetime for when you pass away.

Read this book, and you will learn how to pick the right attorney, make sure all your issues are addressed, and not mess things up for your loved ones. Don't "think about it tomorrow." Read this book today.

# PART I

## AN INTRODUCTION TO ESTATE PLANNING

# IT'S NOT ABOUT THE MONEY

## (BUT IT IS ABOUT THE MONEY)

———

Are you sitting down?

I'm afraid I have some rather shocking news for you.

Take a deep breath. Ready? Here goes: when you die, your stuff is not going with you.

None of it.

Not your house. Not your car. Not your bank accounts. Not your 401(k). Not your cabin by the lake. Not your boat on the lake. Not the artwork on your walls. Not your kids' memorabilia you keep in boxes. Not your fishing rods. And not your Italian bicycle.

Probably not even your signed Babe Ruth baseball.

I'm serious. Lots of people over the millennia have tried to take stuff with them. Vikings piled stuff on funeral boats and set them on fire. Pharaohs stacked stuff in pyramids. As far as we know, these efforts didn't work out.

But here's the thing: all your stuff will not just disappear, either.

Your stuff will go to someone, somewhere, somehow. You may not have made a plan for where it will go, but someone will have a plan—guaranteed. The state you live in will step forward with its specific laws. An ex-spouse will step in with a lawyer.

Even more important than what happens to your stuff is what happens to your minor children and/or dependents who are disabled. If you don't decide who will assume responsibility for them in the event of your death, someone else will.

Someone other than you will stand up in a courtroom, and a judge who you don't know will determine if and how your assets will help the next generation. A set of laws you have likely never read will decide whether your surviving loved ones end up fighting in that courtroom over everything from custody of your children and dependents, to control of your bank accounts and possession of your Italian bicycle.

## NO PLAN? MAYBE YOU'LL GET LUCKY

Now it's possible that everything will go just fine *without* you making a plan. It may be that your state's laws and processes just happen to align with your wishes and the exact configuration of your family at the time you pass on. It may be that everyone involved will approach the situation with the right attitude, the right knowledge, and the time to move your stuff from point A to point B. Maybe they will move it just the way you'd have liked it to move. But believe me: as a living trust and estate planning attorney with a big practice, I deal with this every day. Without a plan, everything rarely goes "just fine."

The odds are high that a lengthy legal process will ensue and damage your surviving family members' relationships.

The odds are very high.

Time and again surviving children tell me that the last memory, sometimes the *lasting memory* they have of their parent is "all that crap we had to go through when Dad died."

Sorry, take a second deep breath, because there's more.

I'm also nearly certain that another dramatic event will happen long *before* you die. If you're like 80 percent of Americans, you will pass through a period of incapacity before you are gone.

If you have a stroke tomorrow and cannot handle your own affairs, *someone* will make medical decisions for you. *Someone* will take control of your portfolio. *Someone* will take over the maintenance of your house. *Someone* will make choices for your minor children and dependents, while you are lying in a hospital or nursing home. And yes, *someone* will have to pay for that nursing home.

Maybe you think you know who that responsible person will be, even if you don't write your wishes down. But suppose your spouse dies before you, or is incapacitated. Suppose your trusted eldest daughter has decided to move to a commune in India. Suppose your kids can't agree on who will handle all those heavy tasks and temptations. Suppose they get into a fight about how to proceed with your medical care. What if they have screaming arguments about whether to try that risky procedure or withhold care? Suppose the state steps in. Or social workers. Or the courts.

Okay, you can exhale now. I'm getting to the good news.

And seriously, there's plenty of good news.

You see, unlike our ancestors over the millennia, and unlike people in less-free countries—that is, most countries—Americans can exercise amazing control over what happens when they die or become incapacitated.

In France, for example, they follow a tradition of *usufruct*. Within that tradition, if you are married, the state basically forces you to give some of your marital property to your children when you die. You really have no option of not giving anything to your children, no matter what your current relationship with them may be.

In this great nation of ours, you will find surprising respect for the wishes of the deceased and incapacitated—as long as those wishes are recorded on the right documents, follow the local laws, assets are properly structured, and responsible people follow through on the plan.

We have a process to make this work that's complex and imperfect, but probably better than any similar process in history.

The process works as long as you have an estate plan.

If you have a plan, you really can make things come out for the best—or at least, as nearly as possible to the way you would have wanted. Life is like that, and so, I'm telling you, is death.

What's an estate plan?

An estate plan is a vital collection of legal documents that include a living trust, a will, durable powers of attorney for property and healthcare, a "HIPAA" authorization, a living will, deeds, beneficiary designations on life insurance, annuities, IRAs, 401(k)s, and sometimes more.

A real plan must be drafted by a lawyer, and it requires constant updating and revision. It's not a downloadable, cookie-cutter document, and it's not done once and forgotten.

No plan? We're pretty much always talking major mess.

Trouble is, lots of Americans—actually most Americans—don't want to hear the shocking news I just asked you to read. At some level, they just don't believe it's true. And as a result, they don't exercise their rights and freedoms. They don't make any plan of consequence. Indeed, 55 percent die without even a will. Then, when the truly inevitable happens, their lack of planning often causes genuine catastrophes in their families.

Arguments. Chaos. Life disruption. Loss of jobs by overwhelmed spouses, children, and other loved ones. Minors placed with the wrong relatives or in foster care. Years in courtrooms for the rich and poor alike.

Believe me, I see such catastrophes every week. I have plenty of stories about people who die without wills or trusts, or get very ill without setting up powers of attorney.

For now, however, let's get back to that good news, because here's the simple message of this book: If you avoid the usual big blunders that most Americans make in planning the succession of their estates, you will not just leave your assets to whom you want in the way you want to, but you will leave a *legacy*. The time of your passing or incapacity will be guided by common sense, fairness, logic, and your best intentions—instead of chaos, strife, and uncertainty. And you will *know* that you have been a genuine help to your loved ones as they move forward with their lives.

It can be done.

Let me explain the title of this Introduction: *It's Not about the Money (but It Is about the Money)*. I wanted to start with that phrase, because although our values and relationships are certainly more important than our money, the way we use and pass on money reflects our values, and can help embody our relationships, our loves, our accomplishments, our intentions, and our legacy. As adults, many of us have learned the following hard lesson:

*Doing money right usually means doing a lot of other things right.*

In fact, when I hear people say, "It's not about the money," alarm bells go off in my head. Somewhere along the line, I know it definitely *will* be about the money.

Is this a do-it-yourself estate planning book? No. I've written a short book on a complex subject, because I think it is literally impossible to teach you to do this yourself. Situations are too varied. The laws and priorities keep changing. The stakes are too high, and the pitfalls too large for you to avoid using an attorney to help with your estate plan. *Period.*

But this book will help you understand the *big picture* of estate planning and empower you to move forward with confidence. I want to get you past the denial and paralysis that plague most people approaching this subject. I want to help you pick the *right* attorney, and make sure he or she is covering *all the bases*. I want to ensure that you *stay on top* of your situation and leave the legacy you want and deserve.

I've given hundreds of estate planning lectures to thousands of people. Along the way, I've learned that the best way to empower folks is to focus on a simple "Top 10." That is, the Top 10 Mistakes people make in planning the succession of their estates. After reading this book, I want you to work closely with an attorney. And I want you to use this little book to stay prepared, informed, and aware of the key questions every time you enter his or her office.

Most of all, I want my readers to stop making the big mistakes. I want to see happier families. Joyful legacies. Less time in courtrooms. Less taxes paid. Peace among children, parents, siblings, and spouses.

Each of the chapters in Part Two covers one of the "10 Big Mistakes." You can skip around, but for a full understanding, I strongly suggest reading them in order.

At the end of the book, you'll also find a handy checklist of the key issues you and your attorney need to address as you build out your estate plan.

## WHAT YOU DON'T KNOW

There's a well-known pie chart I like to use when I lecture about estate planning. It shows how the biggest dangers in life come not from "what you don't know" but from "what you don't know you don't know."

If you *know* you don't know something, you can get help from the people who do. You can deal with your ignorance. But if you *don't know what you don't know,* you guarantee trouble. For example, you may not know how to change the oil in your car, or even that oil needs changing, but if you don't know that *engines need regular maintenance of some kind,* your car will definitely leave you stranded somewhere, someday.

If the biggest slice of *your* pie lies on the left side of this chart, it's not a good sign.

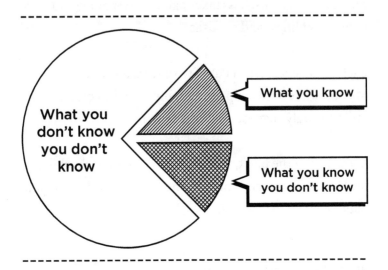

In this little book, I hope to increase "what you know" as much as I can. But I'm certain I can increase "what you know you don't know" by a significant measure. And maybe I can reduce your dangerously large slice of the pie—the entire "what you don't know you don't know" piece—nearly to zero.

By learning the Top 10 Mistakes and using my simple check-list, I want you to have peace of mind. I want you to go to sleep each night—or head out skydiving—knowing that none of the big questions regarding your estate have been left undiscussed. And you absolutely "know what you don't know."

Keep the checklist handy when you speak to your attorney. Scribble on it. If you don't want to write in the book itself, you can easily photocopy the last few pages and carry them around to meetings.

Before we go any further, however, I need to give you more of the big picture.

## ALL TOO OFTEN

Here are the kinds of scenarios that play out in my world all too often.

### SCENARIO #1

My office phone rings, and an anxious male voice comes on the line. "I want to talk to someone about an estate plan for my dad," he says.

"Of course," my receptionist replies. "Can you put your dad on the phone, or can we book him for an appointment?"

"Well, no, he died last night."

"Oh, I'm so sorry."

"Is it too late for an estate plan?" asks the man.

The answer, sadly, is yes. Yes, it's too late. It's also too late if Dad has become sick and mentally incapacitated. Now, we must tell this grieving son that he is likely headed to court. We have to explain that even as he plans the funeral, he needs to start finding out everything he doesn't know about his dad's assets and obligations, past marriages, the works. If the resulting issues are complicated, the surviving son is also now looking at big legal fees.

## SCENARIO #2

I'm at the hair stylist. When she finds out what I do for a living, she says, "Oh, my goodness. Last week one of our good friends, forty-seven-years old, goes to work, isn't feeling well, and heads to the doctor at lunch time. The doctor says, 'Oh, you've just got indigestion.' Well, he's on his way back to work, pulls over, has a heart attack, and dies that afternoon. Boom. Forty-seven-years old! He left a wife and three kids."

"Do you think he had a will or anything?"

"Well, he was only forty-seven," she says.

As she cuts my hair, I'm thinking: If this man and his wife created no estate plan, she will have to turn over every single piece of paper in their lives. Every little rock. Every little pebble. She will have to flip over every little leaf and find out whose name was on that rock, that pebble, that leaf. If she finds only the husband's name on a document, that document will become a problem. She will have to find a process for every single thing she thought they owned together.

I don't say this aloud to my hair stylist, but I know that contrary to popular assumptions, without a proper estate plan, *the wife may not end up with all his assets.* These may go partly to the children. If this happens, and the children are all minors, she may have to set up three guardianships to protect their assets. That's three other legal processes. Suddenly, one legal process morphs into four.

The words ring in my ears: "Well, he was only forty-seven."

**SCENARIO #3**

Recently, a woman I'll call Valerie lost her eighty-three-year-old father to a stroke. One day he's fine, planning a vacation, even; then he doesn't feel well. Two days later, he's dead, without an estate plan. The man was active and healthy, but it was his time. At fifty-five, Valerie has her own family and career. But because of immense hassles associated with her father's affairs—hassles her elderly mother simply cannot handle—Valerie cuts back to part-time work, puts her career on ice, reduces her time with her kids, and moves closer to her mom to care for her. A complete upheaval of her life. For what? The natural death of a father in his eighties.

When I talked to Valerie, I asked myself: Would an estate plan have prevented all of that difficulty? No. But it certainly would have made her life easier. I'm pretty sure her life would not have been turned upside down so completely. In fact, I'm absolutely sure.

## SCENARIO #4

A man in his sixties dies suddenly. His wife assumes that everything they own is marital property. But then she discovers that only his name appears on the deed to a large piece of land he purchased before their marriage. It was never his intention to keep this from her. In fact, he probably never even considered the possibility that she had no ownership rights to the parcel. But now, she has to file a petition in court to get control of this property. Thousands of dollars and several years later, the issue remains unresolved.

## SCENARIO #5

The focus of this book is on estate *planning,* but my law firm also does a lot of litigation work on estate *issues* for heirs. In one case I'll never forget, a woman came in and said, "You know, I'm having a problem."

"I'm sorry to hear that. Let's see how we can help."

"My brother says I threw away his Howdy Doody doll."

"I'm sorry, what did you say?"

"Remember Howdy Doody, the puppet on the 1950s TV show? My brother had a Howdy Doody doll when he was a kid. Apparently, it was in Mom and Dad's garage in a box, like, forever. They've both passed away now."

"And?"

"My brother now claims this doll got thrown away when I went through their stuff. But I never saw any Howdy Doody doll. He claims it was worth $15,000."

I raise my lawyerly eyebrows and say, "Okay, okay. Let's see what we can do."

We go through the court machinations. It's an enormous muddle. And guess what? Right about the time my client hits $15,000 in fees to me, the brother settles. Basically, the brother doesn't care about getting the money. He just wants to inflict $15,000 worth of damage on his sister, because she so "thoughtlessly threw away" his Howdy Doody doll.

They no longer talk to each other. In fact, they hate each other.

Now, maybe they hated each other all along, like Cain and Abel. But maybe there was a way to prevent the Biblical drama from reaching this truly awful point. Perhaps, if their parents had asked whether either of them had valuable childhood possessions they wanted put aside for them, and then specifically called out those possessions in a will, it might have gone better. Maybe if the parents had labeled a box, "Keeping for our son," or separately identified the Howdy Doody doll, it might have been awarded to him in the estate.

If there had been a *plan*, maybe this brother and sister might still, at least, be civil with each other.

### WHAT IS AN ESTATE PLAN, *EXACTLY?*

Earlier I started listing some of the documents that make up a complete estate plan. Let's get into a little more detail now.

We can start by saying that a "last will and testament" does *not* constitute an estate plan. Your will is a document in which you specify what you hope will happen after you die. Your will is *not even a legally binding document* until a state court judge makes a court order that the will is a valid, last will. Prior to that, it's just paper. After you are gone, everyone will read your will and give it weight. But the laws of your state, a judge, and a possibly lengthy legal process will decide what *actually happens.*

As noted, a true "estate plan" is a larger set of documents that includes a will, but offers you far more power. Crucially, a properly constructed plan protects your estate and your wishes *even while you are living.* It determines who cares for you if you can't care for yourself. It gives you and your spouse or other loved one power to protect yourselves and help one another in a variety of extreme situations. When you die, it determines not just *who* inherits your property, but *when* they inherit and in *what manner.* A true estate plan also decides who has guardianship of your minor children, and who takes care of your dependent and disabled loved ones.

Just as importantly, a good estate plan will determine who is in charge at each phase of these processes. It will include custom-designed failsafe mechanisms, like "trust protectors," to guard against unforeseen circumstances, including changes of trustees due to incapacity, or irresponsible heirs destroying your legacy before it has a chance to do any good. (See Mistake #9: Assuming All Trusts Are the Same.)

A good estate plan will minimize the tax burden on your heirs. In other words, it will be tailored not just to *your* specific circumstances, but to *their* specific circumstances.

And yes, the right plan offers the best possible protection against the expensive, debilitating legal processes known as "probate" that cause grief to loved ones, and often waylay people's best intentions. (See Mistake #10: Letting Your Family Go to Probate.)

An estate plan will also keep your legacy organized. I cannot tell you how difficult and burdensome it has become for many heirs to find all the documentation pertaining to their deceased loved ones' bank accounts, debts, business agreements, deeds, outstanding court orders, internet and social media accounts, etc. And don't get me started about paper stock certificates—losing those can lead to a truly expensive mess (see Mistake #3).

Making estate planning decisions and properly crafting the language of the related documents is not, however, a "cut-and-paste" process. As I will repeat again and again, every situation presents different challenges, and every good estate plan will be different from every other. As you learn more, I'm sure you will see why.

### WHO NEEDS AN ESTATE PLAN?

Every adult should have an estate plan. It's that simple. Even an eighteen-year-old should have a signed power of attorney giving someone the right to make healthcare decisions for him or her in case of disability.

I firmly believe that any adult with children, or any adult with any assets that may be of significant importance to surviving family, is being outright irresponsible if he or she does not have a plan.

People wrongly assume that only the rich need estate plans. Let me say this clearly: *your responsibility has absolutely nothing to do with being rich or poor.* If you are living paycheck to paycheck, on minimum wage, an estate plan may be *more* important to the person who inherits your car, your furniture, etc., than it would be to the already-wealthy heir to a multimillion dollar fortune.

Suppose you are indigent, and have children. Did you know that if you pass while they are minors, those children will become eligible for Social Security assistance? As of this writing, this averages out to $1,600 a month for one child, or $3,600 for three children. This means that if you do not designate a guardian for your children, it is not inconceivable that your relatives will argue over not only physical guardianship, but the opportunity to share in that income.

If you don't have an estate plan, you are leaving all of this to chance.

Suppose you are literally homeless, and living under a bridge. Surely, you care who will make healthcare decisions for you when you become incapacitated and unable to act for yourself. Remember, there's an 80 percent chance of that happening at some point.

## THE LIVING TRUST

For most of my clients, at the center of their estate plan sits a document known as a "living trust." Sometimes, attorneys will create separate living trusts for spouses, and sometimes joint trusts, depending on their circumstances and state of residence. This type of trust is called "living," because it goes into effect and protects you even while you are alive. It also lives on past your own death, and in some cases, beyond the death of your immediate heirs. Think of it as a "super will."

A living trust is a legally defined "bucket" into which you place certain kinds of assets so that you and your "successor trustees" have control over those assets. A living trust anticipates your incapacity and death and puts into place your long-term wishes. A living trust is not a legal fiction, but a well-recognized mechanism in an American society that has proven itself time after time to be the best way to plan your estate and protect your legacy for the people and causes you care about.

During your lifetime, you have complete control over this bucket. But, when you become incapacitated or die, a living trust can be easily handed to the next generation.

We'll learn a lot more about living trusts as we go along. For now, you should simply know that every living trust is controlled by a *trustee,* and that trustee will probably be *you* while you are alive. It also has a *beneficiary,* and again, that beneficiary is probably *you* (or you and your spouse) while you live. When you die, the trustees and beneficiaries are updated in an orderly fashion, and the trust moves forward in time without the need for courts.

Most people have heard of living trusts. But in this book, you will find out *what you don't know you don't know* about them, and become empowered to build out your own correctly.

## DURABLE POWERS OF ATTORNEY FOR PROPERTY AND ADVANCED HEALTHCARE DIRECTIVES (DURABLE POWERS OF ATTORNEY FOR HEALTHCARE)

Other crucial documents in an estate plan include "durable powers of attorney." Those powers that pertain to property say, "If I get sick, such-and-such persons have a continuing (durable) power to take care of things that *aren't* in my trust bucket. This person can collect a registered letter from the post office on my behalf, pay my bills, and choose a nursing home for me. This other person can make decisions for my business and my financial holdings. This third person can deal with my IRA, 401(k), 403(b), digital assets, Facebook page, Twitter feed, blog, Instagram, Dropbox, and other social media accounts."

More documents grant advance healthcare directives and "durable powers of attorney for healthcare decisions" when you are unable to make those decisions for yourself. Should the doctor try that new operation? Continue chemotherapy? These documents can have different names in different states, like "advanced healthcare directive" or "physician's directive."

Scary subjects? Maybe. But again, if you don't decide who to entrust with these decisions, someone else will. Why? Because the *decisions will have to be made,* even if you are just out of action for a few hours on the operating table.

## THE LIVING WILL

Most people are familiar with the concept of a "living will" (not to be confused with a "living trust"). A living will states your desires in case of truly extreme medical situations. As with the other documents, your attorney can discuss specific issues with you in detail. Think of a living will as a permission slip that you give your loved ones to let you go when it's your time. But, you may want to say a lot more than, "If I'm a goner, pull the plug."

If you make sure your living will has a way of getting into the right hands at the right time, its instructions will be followed by whoever you give a healthcare power of attorney (see below), as well as by your doctors, even if you cannot communicate with them.

## GUARDIANSHIP NOMINATION

Most people care deeply about the future of their minor (under the age of eighteen) children. If you have minor children, it is truly your responsibility to create documents that nominate a guardian if you are dead or are otherwise disabled, as well as a backup if that guardian is unavailable, found to be unsuitable by the court, or declines when the time comes.

Remember, even if you are young and healthy, you may get in a car accident or suffer another life-ending or disabling disaster. If that happens, social services may pick up your children and kick off a court process to appoint a guardian for them. If you have nominated a guardian in your estate plan, it's very likely (though not guaranteed) that the court will follow your wishes. A judge will decide if the person you have nominated in your will or guardianship documents is suitable. The court will order background and criminal checks on the guardian, and if the person you nominated proves unsuitable, the court will not appoint the person you nominated. They will appoint someone else as guardian, or put your children into the foster care system.

Importantly, guardianship comes in two flavors: *Physical custody* is one kind of guardianship. This is a guardianship of a person. The other is *guardianship of the estate.* This is a guardian in charge of the money. Courts generally separate these two responsibilities, and you may separate them in your estate plan.

Remember, if you do not appoint guardians of the person and estate, the state will. In some states, once a child reaches the age of fourteen or so, he or she can file a petition with the court saying, "Hey, I can live on my own. I've got a job. I don't need a guardian." If your child is likely to take such an action, you may especially want to separate the guardianship of your estate's finances from his or her control. Few teenagers are actually capable of handling their own finances.

Assignment of financial guardianship may also be necessary for older children. If you have a healthy, but clearly irresponsible thirty-five-year-old child, I also feel strongly that your responsibility as a parent does not end with your death, and should be reflected in your estate plan. For example, you may want to designate a trustee to provide a monthly stipend to a troubled adult child, instead of a lump sum.

Even an otherwise responsible and fully capable young person may need a more responsible financial guardian. In most states, beneficiaries gain full access to their inherited assets when they turn eighteen. This can lead even a good kid to trouble. I've seen more than one eighteen-year-old male suddenly inherit $100,000 and immediately go out and buy a fancy sports car for himself. I've seen eighteen-year-old females buy fancy sports cars for their boyfriends. Believe me, it's common. In my experience, few eighteen-year-olds are adept at handling finances.

Another estate planning issue arises when making arrangements for dependents with disabilities. Something like fifty million Americans have some type of disability, which is a significant proportion of the population. Many of my clients have children who are disabled or children with special needs. Sometimes, they were told when their child was born, "This child won't live past twenty-five." Well, now the clients are in their eighties, the children are in their fifties, and the parents are thinking, "What happens to my son or daughter if something happens to me?"

Such decisions may prove agonizing, but no one can choose people to take physical and financial care of your children better than you can. Just as important, the plan must make provision for changes in who cares for your loved one if needed down the line. We'll deal more with those kinds of changes when we talk about "trust protectors" in Mistake #2: Forgetting to Keep Up with Changes and Not Staying in Touch. These and other complexities of guardianship assignment can be dealt with only in a well-crafted estate plan, not a simple "last will and testament."

## MORE DOCUMENTS YOU JUST HAVE TO HAVE

In the Estate Planning Issues Checklist at the end of this book, you will find a more complete list of documents you may want to create during the estate planning process with your attorney. These include:

A "pour-over will" that leaves everything that may not be *in* your trust at death (but should be) *to* your trust. For example, if a lender requires you to take your home out of your trust to refinance the mortgage and you forget to transfer the property back into the trust by deed, your will is there to make sure that the home is distributed under the terms of the trust, rather than your state's laws of intestacy.

A pour-over will is a deed that typically transfers your real property to your living trust. After you create your legal "bucket," you have to move your stuff into it.

A HIPAA (Health Insurance Portability and Accountability Act) authorization allows designees access to your healthcare documents. Think about how important such a document might be. You might not want a home health worker making medical decisions for you, but you might want him or her to be able to pick up a lab report and talk to a nurse about your care. If no such authorization exists, you are definitely creating an unnecessary problem for your own well-being. You don't want vital healthcare information withheld from people who need it in order to help you, simply because you didn't take a little time to get this document in order.

More documents will be created, depending on your specific circumstances. The important thing to remember is that an "estate plan" is not one document, but a collection of appointments, nominations, and directives that determine who will do what, and how your stuff will move from point A to point B. This is not a simple or static collection of documents, but one that must be properly created, maintained, and updated over time.

No estate plan? Not even a will? This is called "intestate succession." Believe me, even though you are gone, you don't want your heirs to go through that kind of succession. Intestate succession generally requires a probate proceeding to settle the estate, and it is certainly no way to leave a viable legacy. In Mistake #10, I will explain, in detail, why probate should be avoided whenever possible.

## DO I REALLY NEED AN ATTORNEY?

At least once a week, I hear the question, "Do I really need to hire an attorney? Can't I just get a do-it-yourself book or web service, or simply Google this stuff and figure it out on my own?"

Let me put it this way: imagine that you want to make mushroom stew for your children. You have a book that says, "Out in the forest you will find many strangely colored mushrooms. Here are the mushrooms you should eat and here are the mushrooms you should not eat. You take a walk through the forest with your nifty book and your basket, and you pick out mushrooms. Not all the mushrooms are described in the book, so you might have to guess on a few. But you do your best. Then you go home and cook up this great mushroom stew for your children. You smile. You invite them to the table. And you serve it to them.

The mushroom stew may be a brutal analogy, but I'm sorry, it's absolutely relevant. *You really don't know what you don't know* when you go into the forest, and some of the uninformed decisions you make can do a lot of unintended damage to your children and their relationships with one another. Real damage. You wouldn't go mushroom picking without an expert, and you should not create an estate plan without one either.

In fact, every good attorney knows that he or she should have a *different* attorney prepare their personal estate plan. As the great lawyer, Abraham Lincoln, once said, "He who represents himself, has a fool for a client." The same can be said of physicians, who are famous for misdiagnosing their own illnesses. You need an outside, unemotional opinion in matters of great personal importance.

"Sure," you may say, "I know that any one book might not have all the information I need. That's why I go to the internet! It's all there, and people update the sites."

Let me offer a second analogy. Suppose you go to Google and type, "My car won't start." You will get about 150 million results, but you won't get an answer. Why? Because you haven't asked the right question. You simply don't know enough to. If you open Google and type, "How do I replace the timing belt on my 1962 Volkswagen 1600cc Dual ICT Weber?" you're going to find half a dozen videos on YouTube created by gearheads just for that problem. And yes, you are going to figure out how to do it yourself.

But you had to know just the right question to ask Google in the first place.

Just like "My car won't start, what do I do?" the question "How do I create an estate plan?" is simply too broad. Unless you are an attorney, you are no more likely to know that your car is a '62 VW with a timing belt, or that such belts need replacing, than you are to know that you may need an IRA Stretch Trust in addition to your living trust. (See Mistake #5: Assuming Your Living Trust Covers Things Like IRAs, 401(k), 403(b)s, 457s, Annuities, and Insurance.)

If you go on the internet and search, "Intestate Succession, Michigan" you can certainly read all the related laws and get a lot of information about how to deal with a death in that state that includes no will. But reading the laws is not going to get you very far. For starters, you will get lost in legalese, and you will find cross-references to half a dozen related laws that may or may not apply. Furthermore, those laws change all the time.

But again, and much more importantly: *you won't know what you don't know.*

The subject of living trusts alone is highly complex. There are many types of trusts. Trusts for single people. Trusts for married people. Trusts for people from Michigan and trusts for Californians. In the same way, there are many kinds of powers of attorney, and many pitfalls in creating them. (See Mistake #9: Assuming All Living Trust Plans Are the Same.)

Part of my job as a lawyer is winnowing down what's appropriate to my clients' situations and needs. Often, this is similar to a physician prescribing a drug. Often, people come to me thinking they know what they need, just as they go to a physician and say, "I've got a cough, give me some antibiotics." The physician knows that you might have a virus that's untreatable by antibiotics, and he or she will look to see if the cough might be a symptom of something deeper. That's their job.

## THE DANGER OF DIY ONLINE SERVICES

After I tell people they really shouldn't try to do their own estate planning, they inevitably argue back, "But what about those do-it-yourself *online services* for estate planning?"

I know some of you will be tempted to rely on internet services or software packages that promise to automatically generate your estate plan based on questions you answer via an electronic form. But there's a clear and present danger here. The people who create these services know enough to say *right in their ads* that they are not providing any actual legal services. They also know enough *not to say* it's truly impossible to create computer algorithms that deal with all the individual situations that arise, or ask laypeople the questions that will reveal the *hidden issues* impacting the important decisions they need to make.

Life is just not that simple.

What you are really buying through these services is fancy cut-and-paste word processing. You could save their fee just by downloading and modifying sample documents for your state. Again, this should be fine as long as you don't mind gathering those mushrooms for your children's stew by yourself.

If you've created your own estate plan by cutting and pasting from an existing template, or by filling in the blanks of an online program, I would urge you to at least have it reviewed by an expert.

True story: A fellow walks into my office and wants "just a half hour of my time" to review a *one-page* living trust he created himself from a template. One page? These things usually run eighty pages or more. And guess what? They run that long not because legalese is silly, or because "lawyers try to make everything complicated," but because a living trust tries to anticipate the real complexities of life and make everything *absolutely and indisputably clear.* Legalese is not BS. It's about removing ambiguity.

I read this fellow's one-page document and say, "You've already given all your property to your siblings."

"What? No, I didn't," he says.

I hold up the paper. "Look, that's what the document says right here. You give your brothers and sisters everything. Right now."

Finally, he grabs the paper, reads the paragraph aloud, and says with a laugh, "Oh, I didn't even read this. I just pulled it off the internet, filled it out and signed it."

He really had unintentionally given away his property to his siblings before he even died.

As important as unintentional mistakes, is the lack of meaningful discussion with an expert about some of the most important decisions you will ever make in your life. When you use a do-it-yourself program, you are not receiving any kind of counseling from someone who has done this before.

The following is an example of the counsel you will get from someone who has seen hundreds of succession situations play out in real life.

Suppose you have minor children, and in your estate plan, you have to nominate someone to be their guardian if you and your spouse die before they come of age. No light matter, right? Now, if you are staring at a prompt on a do-it-yourself software tool, you *might* put in the exact right name. On the other hand, if I am sitting down with you, I am going to ask some tough questions, such as:

"Who are you thinking about as guardian for your children?"

"I'm thinking about my best friend, Tom."

"Is there any reason you would *not* want to choose Tom?"

"Well, he's a good person, and he shares our faith."

"But is there any reason you would *not* choose him?"

"Well, he's probably not that good with money."

"Really? Tell me about that."

"Well, he's sort of perpetually broke, and a few years ago, he made some really dumb investments. Some idiot talked him into investing in a platinum mine somewhere. I had to give him a loan to bail him out."

"Ah."

"But he's super caring and otherwise very responsible. And the kids love him to pieces. If we died, we'd leave plenty of money for him to take care of the kids."

In such a case, my advice might be, "Name Tom as guardian of the *person* of the children, but there's no reason not to name someone else as guardian of the *estate*. The guardian of the person will take care of the kids, but this other guardian will watch over the money. All the money will be in your living trust, but the guardian of the *estate* will stand in the financial shoes of the child and make appropriate and responsible financial decisions. There may have to be a little negotiation from time to time between the two guardians regarding how much money is available in any given year, but that may be for the best. Yes, it's true that guardians have been known to sue one another. But, we live in an imperfect world, and separating guardianship in this way may be a better option."

You and I would also discuss a "trust protector"—likely a professional who would be given the power to modify the trust and name new trustees, if necessary.

Another example where tough questions are crucial: Suppose you have grown children. They are all responsible and actively employed. You'd like to divide your estate evenly among them. Terrific. But if I'm sitting with you, I will ask some necessary questions.

"Tell me about your children's marriages," I might ask.

"Well, they're all doing fine except for Suzy. I'm worried that she may be heading for a divorce someday."

"Then let's talk about writing your plan to protect your daughter's inheritance from being lost in a divorce." This is very important, because half the time people will tell me they think their children's marriages are shaky, and guess what? It's not hard to lose much of an inheritance in a divorce, even years after the divorce, depending on how things play out.

*No online program can possibly help you with these kinds of discussions,* or help you figure out how to plan in advance for changing situations in your particular family.

Allow me to just say one more thing about working with an expert.

Part of what each of us faces as we plan our estates is the simple difficulty of grappling with our own mortality. This is understandably daunting, highly emotional, and a big part of the reason even expert attorneys go to someone else to help them plan.

Estate planning is not a kitchen remodeling project. It's not a repair to your Volkswagen. You're going to be preparing documents that lawyers and loved ones are going to be looking at after you are dead and unable to clarify your wishes further. Your estate plan is a heavy responsibility. It deserves your utmost respect and the best advice you can find.

Think about it like this: "I'm signing this document, and after I'm out of action, someone is really going to be looking at this in detail. It will outlive me, and every single word is going to matter."

### WHAT IF I ALREADY HAVE A PROFESSIONAL ESTATE PLAN?

Remember, even if your estate plan was well crafted by a qualified attorney, it was only a snapshot in time.

Do you now live in a different state? Have more children? Was there a divorce in the mix? Our lives are complex and highly changeable. When I think of my own life ten years ago, I am astounded at how much has changed. I'm living 400 miles away, I've had three different houses, and my wife and I adopted two children. The list goes on and on.

Now, not only did my life change over the last decade, but, I assure you, the laws did too.

Every week, people come into my office and say, "Mom and Dad did this estate plan thirty years ago, and they died. Here you go." I take a look, and often my first questions have to be, "Tell me what changed in the last thirty years." Not surprisingly, this is often a lot. I hear about births, deaths, separations, purchases of real estate, and moves to other countries that make the existing plan very difficult or impossible to implement—and much more likely to end up in probate court.

Simply put, most estate plans are *backward looking*. They deal with the family events which have already happened, not those which might possibly happen in the future. Only the rare estate plan is *future looking,* which means it was created by an expert attorney with language to account for possible changes in the future.

Bottom line: read this book and then have a qualified attorney review your existing plan.

## CHOOSING AN ATTORNEY

Now that you've made the wise choice to look for an estate planning attorney, you will not be surprised to learn that all attorneys are not created equal.

For starters, you need to know that we have two kinds of lawyers in this country: general purpose and special purpose. If you live in a large urban setting, you will have no difficulty finding someone who focuses on estate planning law. If you live in a rural setting, it may be tough to find someone who does estate planning more than a few times a year. Why? Because in a rural setting, attorneys have to provide general services just to make a living.

In larger states, you may also find a certified specialist program. In California, for example, I'm a certified specialist in estate planning, trust, and probate law. To receive that certificate, a lawyer must have been in practice for at least five years, have handled a certain number of estate cases, and then pass an additional full-day bar exam (beyond the two- or three-day bar exam lawyers must pass in order to practice law). There's also a background reference check with other lawyers and judges to make sure we know what we are doing. It's pretty rigorous. And in states where such certifications exist, having that certificate on the wall means a great deal. In California, less than half of 1 percent of (or one in 200) lawyers are certified specialists in estate planning, trust, and probate law.

Now, this does not mean just because your attorney is not a certified specialist, he or she doesn't have adequate capabilities. A smaller state may not even have these particular certification programs. But if you can find a certified specialist, it does mean that the State Bar has given that lawyer an extra stamp of approval. They're likely to know what they're doing.

## "TELLS" OF A GOOD ATTORNEY

Poker players look for "tells" to see if the other players have a good hand, or are only bluffing. If an attorney specializes in estate planning, trust, and probate law, that's a good sign. If estate work makes up all, or nearly all of his or her firm's business, that's a good tell, indeed.

But, if you're interviewing an attorney and he tries to impress you with his range of expertise by bragging that he handled a criminal case at 8:30 a.m., a divorce at 10:00 a.m., an immigration case at 2:00 p.m., and now he's doing your estate plan at 4:30 p.m., that's a bad tell, and you should look elsewhere. If you're living in a more rural area, you might have to travel a bit to find a focused expert.

Does the focus of the attorney really matter that much? *Yes. It's a sad fact that most attorneys lack the depth of knowledge required for even a simple estate plan.* Indeed, most attorneys will likely go to the internet and download a template just like you would. Shocking, but true. This challenging, rapidly shifting area of law requires a highly specialized expertise most attorneys simply do not possess.

Of course, mere specialization may not be enough. For example, many estate planning attorneys know very little about income tax law, which every year becomes more and more important to my clients and their heirs. Remember, it's not what you make, or what you pass on, it's what all of you keep. Income taxes can take a huge bite out of your estate, both now and after you die. And it's easy to accidentally create huge tax headaches for your beneficiaries. This is especially true for wealthy heirs, who have to engage in a careful balancing act with the IRS each year.

Bottom line: be sure to probe a potential attorney deeply about income tax planning expertise. Consider this another important tell.

Many people now have much of their money in IRAs. As you will learn in Mistake #5, the arcane rules regarding IRA distributions make this an extremely complex area of estate planning. I am regularly shocked by the ignorance of some colleagues in these issues.

The tell? Make your attorney explain the Federal IRA Minimum Distribution Table found in Publication 590b Appendix B Table I Single Life Expectancy (see Mistake #5) and the consequences for your heirs. If he or she can't do this off the top of their head, it's a bad sign.

Another bad sign: the attorney doesn't ask for a detailed

list of your assets *before* he or she starts writing your estate plan. Different kinds of assets, such as IRAs and annuities, require very different treatment. For example, as we will learn in Mistake #5, IRAs do not go into living trusts.

Attorneys must also articulate a process for reviewing your estate plan regularly, including your assets. Many attorneys "write it and forget it," but the failure to make regular updates to your plan ranks right up there at Mistake #2.

What about the physical age of the attorney? Is that another tell?

People often think that the older we lawyers are, the more experience we must have. Partly true, I suppose. But frankly, I find it more important to stay current in the estate planning field. That means belonging to the right associations, reading the right publications, going to the right seminars. I probably spend six or seven hours a week—almost a full day—week in and week out, learning new laws, techniques, and approaches, and then teaching the nuances of estate law to our internal staff.

Five years of actual practice is probably enough if the attorney is an active specialist, especially a certified specialist who stays up to date. Someone with thirty years of experience may or may not be current on the law, the latest tax information, or software aids.

If you choose an older attorney, consider one who is part of a larger firm, which will survive his or her retirement. Certainly, you should ask about the attorney's own succession plan. Who will take over regular plan reviews after their retirement?

Software aids? Wait. Wasn't I ragging on software earlier? But there's software and there's *software*. And then there's the knowledge of how to use it properly. Most modern attorneys use professional software aids to make the process efficient. But we're talking about software with sophisticated algorithms designed for use by attorneys that incorporate relevant searches of case law. Modern attorneys know that professional software, properly utilized, can help them create more highly customized trusts than they can by following manual processes alone.

They also know where the software ends, and the real world begins. If they're good, they take no shortcuts around asking the tough questions.

### ANOTHER TELL: THE FEE STRUCTURE

Yes, it's going to cost you some money to create a solid estate plan and keep it up to date. But if your heirs can avoid probate court (again, see Mistake #10: Letting Your Family Go to Probate), you will likely save them at least ten times your attorney's fees in money and time. Probably more.

But the *way* your attorney charges you can be just as important as the total cost. Will you be charged hourly? For each visit? Each phone call? A yearly fee to keep things up to date? A flat fee of some kind? You won't find any state-based or other types of standards for fees. Attorneys approach billing in different ways. And beyond protecting your wallet, these differences provide another tell.

First, a bit of history. Until a few years ago, direct *estate taxes*—what people called "the death tax"—used to be the big, obvious reason to do an estate plan. Attorneys could charge large hourly fees just for helping you figure out how to dodge the dreaded death tax. (See more in Mistake #4: Relying on Your Living Trust as a Tax Plan.)

Now, thanks to changes in federal and many state laws, fewer and fewer heirs are affected by estate (or "death") taxes. At the same time, however, clients planning their estates are facing a host of new, bigger, and more complex tax issues of their own. Many experienced attorneys have expanded their services to address clients' broader needs, including *detailed income tax planning*, not just for the estates clients are passing on, but for their lives here and now.

The result? Better service for you and a more predictable cost model for the attorney. That means straight hourly charges have become less and less appropriate. Why?

Because firms can package up their work in more efficient ways to keep budgets under control. Technology and assistants can be utilized to keep the planning processes and continuous learning organized—at least by an attorney who specializes in estate planning.

In essence, busy estate attorneys can now spread business risk among multiple engagements. When they charge you for every minute of their time, it means they have transferred all the business risk to you. And it probably means they do not do a high volume of this kind of work.

The tell? Attorneys who offer a higher value proposition for their clients now tend to operate on a flat fee basis. In my firm, we charge a flat fee based on the scope of the planning. We don't charge clients for each phone call or each office visit, and we don't charge for peer reviews of the plan. It's all built in. Even years down the line, if you call and say, "Hey, Johnny got divorced, do I need to change my plan?" we don't charge anything for the consultation, only for actual rewriting.

So, ask your potential attorney if they're going to charge you for every call and conversation. If they do, consider it a sign that he or she has fallen a bit behind the times, and you should probably look for a firm with a more modern, flat-fee approach. (If you have over $10 million in assets to plan, however, and your financial situation is complex, you may expect to be charged for hourly work.)

## ONE MORE TELL: ASSOCIATIONS

Finally, you should do a little research to find out if your attorney is affiliated with one or more legal associations devoted to estate planning work.

For example, I am affiliated with a group called the Wealth-Counsel, which has a sister group, ElderCounsel. These offer highly current seminars, updates, and conferences on estate planning. Only with this kind of diligent and continuous learning can a genuine estate attorney stay up to date and maintain a network of the best minds in the field.

No such affiliations with associations for estate planning? No continuing education program within the firm? Think twice.

## USING THIS BOOK WITH YOUR ATTORNEY

I wish I could tell you that once you've chosen an attorney, your responsibility in this process will come to an end, and you can just go along for the ride.

I wrote this book because your work with your attorney will be far more effective if you know why you're going through all this trouble with him or her. It will be even more effective if you understand some of the underlying issues and pitfalls. After reading this short volume, I hope you will have become more than just a smart consumer of legal help—I hope this will serve as a means of checks and balances on your personal estate planning.

You are *not* going to do this yourself, but you *are* going to make sure it's done right.

If you are an attorney yourself, I hope you will hand this book to clients and say, "Read this little volume, and you will have a better understanding of what we're doing here. Please focus on common Mistakes #6 and #7, so we can talk clearly about your plan."

## A WORD ABOUT LEGACY

What is a legacy? It's not just the stuff you leave behind, not just the life and faith lessons you try to convey, but the stories and memories, too.

Here, I have to offer you another difficult fact of human existence. People often remember the endings of stories better than they remember the beginning or middle.

I meet with many families and I cannot help but tell you that all too often, what they remember best about a parent happened *right before* and *right after* that parent died: the muddle, the arguments with siblings, the legal battles.

Of course, this is not always the case. Some surviving children keep it all in perspective. But many do not. Too often, I hear complaints like the one below.

"I am so upset with my sister, because while Dad was getting sick, she started sucking up all his money 'to take care of him.' And then when Mom died, all of us had that huge argument right in the funeral home. Everyone blew up and went home mad."

Sadly, that's the legacy that often remains. Memories like these can be among the most powerful your children carry through the rest of their lives—more powerful than kinder, gentler memories of you, and of better times when they were young.

Now, few of us *want* to deal with these issues before we die or become disabled. Maybe we don't want the future to interfere with the present. Or maybe our denial arises from our primal fear of death.

But please understand, these issues are not going away. By not dealing with them, you are effectively pushing them onto the people you love, and especially onto the people who love you. They will have to take care of these issues one way or another. And this will be a lot harder if you do no planning. Dealing with your estate will be an added burden and hardship—possibly, an awful one.

Your legacy is at stake, but so is your *parenthood*.

When my mother was eleven years old, she lost her mother. When she was fifty-four, she lost her father. At that time, she said to me, "Well, I'm an orphan now." It was kind of strange to hear a fifty-four-year-old say, "I'm an orphan," but I realized it was true. I saw how we never stop being our parents' children, and our parents never stop playing that role, even after they die.

I believe that properly leaving your legacy—your beliefs, your values, your memories, and yes, your stuff—is part of the *full* life cycle of being a parent. It was one of the responsibilities laid on you when you gave birth.

A related responsibility attaches to being a child. If you are helping your aging parents prepare an estate plan, I think that anticipating the emotional issues for you and your siblings is also part of your responsibility as a son or daughter—*part of the life cycle of being a child.*

Many times, a client has said to me something like, "I know my sister is going to be a problem when my parents die."

"How do you know that?" I ask.

"Because my sister has been a problem my whole life. I'm a responsible adult. I know she is not a responsible adult."

Does being "responsible" include helping your parents

structure an estate plan to avoid the problems you see coming? I think it does.

I was talking with a client the other day who said, "I'm really worried that when Mom and Dad pass away, it's going to hit my brother hard. He's sixty-two and probably has undiagnosed autism. He lives in the same room he had in high school, with the same childhood things in it. He never changed. Probably, if Mom and Dad get sick, or certainly when they die, the house will have to be sold. There's really no other choice. My brother will not be able to continue living in the house, and he won't understand why."

In that case, I think it is up to the responsible child to work with the parents, to get them to understand that if they love their children, they will deal with this situation properly in their estate plan, no matter how hard it is to discuss in the present.

If parents hate their children—well, they can skip the estate plan, and leave a big, stinking mess. That is the brutal, simple truth. By ignoring a complex emotional issue that will *certainly occur upon your death,* you will certainly harm your children.

We should all rejoice that the individual states of the United States have developed tools to make it possible for rich and poor alike to leave a good legacy. These tools can be used to prevent many arguments: to preserve maximum harmony among children, to protect memories and best intentions, and yes, to give the next generation a little help along the road to success.

Let us learn to use those tools and use them well.

# PART II

# THE TOP TEN MISTAKES PEOPLE MAKE WITH THEIR ESTATES

# #10

# LETTING YOUR FAMILY GO TO PROBATE

---

When your kids were little, you wouldn't let them run in the street.

When they were teens, you wouldn't let them stay out until dawn.

When they became adults, you wouldn't let them send money to Nigerian princes soliciting them by email.

And when you die, believe me, you should not let them go to probate court, not if there's anything you can do to prevent it.

But unless you do the right kind of estate planning—which

goes well beyond signing a will—you create an *extremely high probability* that your heirs will go to probate court. In probate, they will have to stand up and *prove* to a judge that they have a right to your property. If you don't divide up those rights clearly in advance, if the names on the title documents are confused or out of date, or if your children encounter a dozen other possible complications, they may well have to lawyer-up and fight over your estate.

Just to get to the point of standing in front of a probate judge, it will take weeks, months, or sometimes years. And the bitterness resulting from a battle among your heirs may last the rest of their lives. In the end, the legal costs may well consume their entire inheritance—it happens often.

Am I exaggerating? Unfortunately, I am not. I have dealt with many estate successions, and stood in probate court many times. I know the deal.

What is probate? It comes from the Latin word *probare*, which means "to try, test, examine, prove." In modern English, we might translate it this way: "unbelievable and unpredictable hassle."

### PROBATE IS *ALWAYS* A HASSLE

Let's take a "simple" case. Bob Sr. dies. He is survived by Bob Jr. and his estranged daughter, Jane. Bob Jr., is lucky enough to locate a signed, properly witnessed, last will and testament that leaves everything to him. A few weeks after the funeral, for which he has paid, Bob Jr. realizes it's time to deal with his inheritance. For starters, the funeral has set him back $6,000, and he could use the money.

At some point during those two weeks, it dawns on Bob Jr. that if he takes no action, he will get nothing. His name does not appear on any of his father's accounts or title documents. After a little research, he discovers that no "inheritance agents" are going to track him down to hand him his father's money, or the deed to his house, or the keys to his safe deposit box.

Now, Bob Jr. needs to get to work.

First, he goes through his father's desk and finds $800 in cash. He puts this in his pocket. So far, so good, he figures. But, in fact, he has just broken the law, because regardless of the will, the cash is not his, and neither he nor his siblings' rights to that cash have been established by a judge.

He also finds a bunch of bank statements. He's not sure if they cover all his dad's bank accounts, but he pulls one from Friendly State Bank, and decides to go meet with them.

Bright and early one Monday morning, Bob Jr. puts on a tie and drives down to the local branch. The Friendly State

Bank manager sits him down in his office, where Bob Jr. pulls out Bob Sr.'s death certificate, along with the signed will, and asks to be given access to his father's account.

"Sorry, sir," says the manager. "We will need letters testamentary from the probate court. We also need a probate court order, which proves that this is the last will your father left behind and that you are the official executor. I'm afraid your father never transferred his accounts here into a living trust."

"Excuse me?" asks Bob Jr.

The bank manager smiles. He sees the look in Bob Jr.'s eyes at least once a week. Hardly anyone knows about such things until they have to know about them—and often, that look of bewilderment is the first hint that these people's lives are about to take a whole new turn. The manager is also smiling, because he knows that Bob Sr.'s money isn't going anywhere soon.

"I'm talking about documents signed by a judge and a clerk of the probate court. You have to petition the court to get them. And make sure they have the official stamp—the purple stamp by the way, not the black one."

"I bet someone is going to ask for those kinds of documents when I try to take title to the house, too."

"Yep."

## THE TROUBLE BEGINS

Now, if Bob Jr. has plenty of time and patience, and makes an effort to learn the ins and outs of probate proceedings, he *may* eventually figure out how to get his letters testamentary. But, he is about to enter into a very frustrating and archaic process.

He will encounter a series of weird laws and will wait in a lot of long lines.

He will get a pat down from security if he leaves his pocket knife in his pocket as he walks through the airport-style metal detector at the courthouse.

He will discover that the world of the court is nothing like the efficient world of business. For example, he will discover that he will have to complete the probate process in a certain sequence. If he does them in the wrong sequence, the process can come to a screeching halt.

At this point, Bob Jr. might pick up the phone and call a probate attorney to handle the rest of the process. He probably should. For one thing, an attorney might know about exceptions to probate in his state, especially if the assets have a low value. Some states might also offer an abbreviated proceeding. The time an attorney could save Bob Jr. would likely cover his legal fees.

Most likely, however, Bob Jr. won't call an attorney yet, because he still doesn't know what he's getting into. He's a babe in the woods.

Bob Jr. does a little research and finds out that he has to go down to the probate clerk's office to kick off the process. There, a clerk hands him about eight forms and says, "You need to petition the court. You will be the petitioner. It's very simple. Here's a four-page form, a three-page form, and some two-page and one-page forms. Please fill everything out correctly and in the proper manner. Pay attention to the sequence of each step. Bring them back when you have everything done, and we'll give you a hearing date." Lawyers have a charming word for this process. We call it a "form pleading."

Bob Jr. learns to his surprise that thanks to probate, he has to publish a notice in a local newspaper telling the world that his dad has passed away. But he's more concerned to learn that he has to notify all of his father's descendants, all of the people named in the will, and *anyone* who would inherit in the absence of a will.

All this must be completed before he can get the papers he needs to take control of his dad's assets.

Now, a chill runs down Bob Jr.'s spine as he suddenly recalls that after his father and mother divorced when the kids were young, Bob Sr. had married a woman in Nevada on a whim. They broke up shortly thereafter. Bob Jr. has no idea even of the woman's name, or if she is alive. After all, his father died at eighty-five, and all that happened long ago. Bob Jr. doesn't know if his dad ever divorced this Nevada woman or not. But now, Bob Jr. has to find out whether they were still married, and whether she is still alive, and notify her.

Then there's Bob Jr.'s own sister, Jane. She and Bob Sr. argued bitterly and haven't spoken in roughly twenty-five years. She was largely left out of the will, save for a box of her old college paraphernalia, and Bob Jr. hasn't had any contact with her for at least a decade. Last he heard, she had moved to Bahrain (or was it Kuwait?) to teach English. Now, he has to notify her, but he doesn't have her address or any way to find it.

Then, Bob Jr. is stunned to discover that in the course of probate, *all* the details of his father's assets will become part of the public record, including full information about his father's possible heirs, including the estranged Nevada wife. This might open up the estate to scam artists, which rightly scares him.

Bob Jr. was named as sole beneficiary in the will. But he

will have to stand in line with everyone else for a chance to make his claim before a judge.

It's lucky that Bob Sr. was fully retired and had no partnership interest in a business. Imagine how complicated *that* would be to unwind. Or, imagine if Bob Sr. had left no will at all, which is true for about 55 percent of Americans. That's right: 55 percent of Americans die "intestate," guaranteeing no end of hassles for their heirs. The numbers are highest among minorities.

## TIME BEGINS TO FLY

As it happens, it takes Bob Jr. only a month to find and send out notices to all the possible heirs, publish the information in a newspaper, fill out all the forms, and get the forms back to the probate court. Like the funeral, this costs a bit of money and time—neither of which he can really afford.

Meanwhile, more bank and investment statements have arrived in his dad's mail. Small accounts, but assets Bob Jr. didn't know about. One's an IRA, which he foolishly considers to be just other asset he can cash out. (For much more on this issue, see Mistake #5: Assuming Your Living Trust Covers Things Like IRAs, 401(k), 403(b)s, 457s, Annuities, and Insurance.)

Then there's the mysterious wife from his dad's past. It

turns out that his dad *never divorced the woman* and she's not dead, which causes Bob Jr. more than a little worry. He sent his sister a notice to her last known address and got no reply. Will these issues somehow mess things up?

When Bob Jr. takes his petition to the court to get a hearing date, he hands all his papers to a clerk, along with a check for the court fees (there are always court fees). The clerk checks to see that all the forms are minimally filled out, and hands Bob Jr.'s petition back with a stamp and a hearing date.

The date is just six weeks away, but Bob Jr. has a problem. "This date doesn't work for me," he says. "I'm going to be out of town."

"I'm sorry, but that is your date. You should have told me before."

Because Bob Jr. has never done this before, he didn't know that before he handed over the petition, he needed to tell the clerk his schedule limitations. If he had negotiated beforehand, he might have gotten a better date. But now he is stuck. Is every courtroom like that? No. But is this typical of the overall probate process he is about to experience in real time? Yes.

Of course, on Bob Jr.'s hearing date, the judge may be sick or called away to a more important matter. Or, the court transcriber might be sick, and the whole thing will be delayed. A lot can go wrong before you get your time in front of a judge, even if your case is straightforward. Even if your parents made a proper will, there's no argument among siblings, and you have done everything just right. (If not, well, see Mistake #7: "Letting Your Beneficiaries Muddle Through on Their Own.")

On the date of the hearing, Bob Jr. leaves for the courthouse with plenty of time to spare. Someone told him to show up an hour-and-a-half early, because if he is not there at the moment his case is called, he will lose his date and will have to start again. But, when he gets to the courthouse, the lot has filled up, and he has to park a couple of blocks away. Then he has to stand in a *very* long line at security—a process that operates similarly to an airport's, only not as efficiently. Then, he gets lost in the huge building. By the time he enters the courtroom, Bob Jr. has only ten minutes to spare before his 9:15 a.m. call time.

Judges are free to lock the doors on people who have a 9:15 a.m. appearance and show up at 9:16 a.m.

A probate court will typically post online or in a paper near the courtroom door, a list of "matters" for the day, along with what are called "probate notes" and "tentative rulings." "Probate notes" are written by court staff to let the judge know what's going on in the case and what may be missing from the file. "Tentative rulings" indicate the way the judge intends to rule. It makes a complex process incrementally more efficient. You can see if your matter has been recommended for approval on the first hearing or not.

If your matter is recommended for approval, you will likely get a court order for your letters testamentary and other documents to be prepared (though of course, not right away). If your matter is recommended to be continued, it's usually because you still need to do a number of things that, in the opinion of the judge, you have so far failed to accomplish.

Bob Jr. gets depressed when he sees that his case has been recommended for continuance. But he still needs to get through this hearing.

Inside the courtroom, our hero blinks at the size of the operation. The room is large, and several dozen people are sitting and waiting for their cases to be called. At the moment, however, nothing seems to be happening, and he learns from someone that the judge was late getting in that morning, and still hasn't appeared on the bench. The judge was supposed to start proceedings at 8:30 a.m. but, well, he's a judge, and he does what he wants.

When the judge appears at 9:30 a.m., the court starts calling cases, or "matters" at a perplexing speed. In Los Angeles County, with its millions of residents, I've seen one hundred matters called in sixty minutes. You do the math. But in a rural county, where the courts have less on their plates, they might call only six matters in a whole day. There's just no way to know.

Bob Jr. watches petitioner after petitioner stand before the bench. The probate judge glances at the papers, looks at the staff recommendation, asks a question or two, and then either approves and signs an order, denies it, or continues the matter. He often makes these decisions in seconds.

At last, around 11:45 a.m., just when Bob Jr. begins to despair that the court will close before his matter is called, he hears his name. He rushes forward.

The judge glances at the stack of papers, eyeballs Bob Jr., and asks, "Where's your sister, Jane?"

"I don't know, your honor. I did send a letter to her last address. My father—"

"Case continued four weeks for service. Next case."

"I'm sorry, your honor, what does that mean and what do I do next?"

"You must file a Proof of Service that states under penalty of perjury that you have mailed a Notice of Petition to Administer Estate to your sister. Next."

"But I don't know where she is."

"Find her. Your case has been continued. I am calling the next matter, and if you do not leave the courtroom, I will have the bailiff escort you out of the building."

With that, Bob Jr.'s shoulders sag, and he leaves the courtroom in a hurry.

If Bob Jr. has all the answers for the court on the next hearing, he *may* get his approval. If not, his case will likely be continued once again. Once he has too many continuances, Bob Jr.'s case will be dismissed, and he will have to start all over again with a new petition.

But let's say Bob Jr.'s matter was not continued, and let's say it was not dismissed. Let's say the judge smiled and said, "All right, Bob Jr., you have done everything you need to do. This is a miracle of miracles. I can't believe it. You are so smart. You were so well prepared. I'm going to sign your order." And the judge signs a court order approving his petition for letters testamentary.

After this positive hearing, a smiling Bob Jr. heads down

to the clerk of the court, who he now knows works on the third floor. He stands in line, and says with good cheer, "The judge just signed my order. Please issue me letters testamentary and other documents the Friendly Bank is asking for."

The clerk smiles back and says, "The order is still with the judge. We have to wait for the file to get down here."

"When does that happen?"

"Sometimes it takes a week or two. Sometimes three or four."

Bob Jr. is thinking, "You've got to be kidding, right?" But of course, he's too smart to say this out loud.

Why does it take so long? You see, even in this digital day and age, courts still shuffle a lot of physical paper. Judges have to return physical files to clerks. Clerks put these on a stack, and then someone in the back office has to review all the paperwork it contains. Your court order is just one of these pieces of paper, which the judge has signed. Your letters testamentary are separate pieces of paper that the clerk signs after he or she makes sure all the language matches up, and the seal can be applied. This takes time.

In the end, a clerk may put the relevant letters in the mail to Bob Jr. or Bob Jr. may have to go back through the metal detectors in the court to pick it all up. It depends on the individual court's process. Assuming all has run quite smoothly, a few months after his father's death, Bob Jr. will get the authority to act. Friendly State Bank will finally get friendly.

But that's not the end of the story. Bob Jr. will have to bring a petition to conclude the probate proceeding once all the work is done. Only after the petition for final distribution is final can Bob Jr. actually distribute his inheritance to himself.

What if the process doesn't run smoothly? As of this writing, *the average probate in California requires sixteen months.* That includes the problem cases that run years, but none runs as short as two months.

Bottom line: it's easy to start probate. It's a lot harder to finish.

## IN MOST STATES, "TITLE CONTROLS"

Without a complete estate plan, even surviving spouses often have to go through long or short versions of probate to get full control of their family's assets. In the meantime, terrible hardships can ensue.

Wait! If your spouse dies—don't you automatically get control of his or her assets, even if no will was signed?

The answer is maybe yes, and maybe no.

In most states, "title controls." This means that if your name is jointly included on the title of the asset, whether a house or a bank account, and the title was structured for joint tenancy with rights of survivorship, the surviving joint tenant will get the account or property. In other words, you, as the survivor, will indeed be given instant control of that asset.

Or not. It depends. Even if all your assets are held as joint tenancy with right of survivorship, what happens when the last man (or woman) dies?

Sometimes joint tenancy and joint ownership have their own pitfalls. Suppose, for example, your spouse has a business bank account that he shares with a business partner. Your spouse dies, it might be the partner—not you—who gets control of that account. You may be on the sidelines yelling, "Hey, that was marital property, I'm entitled to my half of that account." But absent a clear estate plan, you may have to file a probate petition and start a battle that may or may not let you gain control of the disputed assets. The matter will quickly become complicated, and it's likely that lawyers will get involved.

A class of assets which generally avoid probate are: Transfer on Death (TOD), or Payable on Death (POD) accounts.

You will generally see TOD on securities and POD on bank accounts.

If some of Bob Sr.'s money resided in a POD bank account, and he named Bob Jr. as the POD beneficiary to the account, then indeed, Bob Jr. would merely have to show up at that bank with a photo ID and a death certificate in order to gain control of the account. Such accounts do not need to go through probate. In fact, they are not even covered by a will.

This may simplify things, or it may create unintended problems for multiple heirs.

If you are going through life creating some assets that are POD to multiple names, some that are jointly held, some that are inside a living trust (see below), and others that you simply fail to track properly, then you are creating more and more issues for the next generation.

Those issues will have a name: *probate.*

### SOMETIMES, PROBATE IS A NIGHTMARE

Bob Jr. had it easy.

I have plenty of clients for whom the failure to do proper estate planning has led to a true nightmare. Take a couple I will call Katerina and Ivan, immigrants from the Ukraine who have lived much of their adult lives in California. They've become citizens of the United States, and have four kids.

At age forty-eight, Ivan died of a heart attack while driving a truck at work. Katerina's English was poor, so when she came to see me, she brought along a translator, just in case.

Now, it was a mistake, but hardly unusual, for Katerina's forty-eight-year-old husband to have made no will. If Ivan thought about it at all, he probably assumed that under the marital property or "community property" laws of California, his wife would get everything if he died.

Ivan was wrong, for he had made another important succession error.

Shortly before he died, Katerina had run up about $25,000 on her credit card, and the couple worried that they would lose their home to the credit card company. At that point, Ivan said to Katerina, "I'll tell you what. Let's just put the house in my name alone, and that will take care of everything. The credit card company can't take the house if it belongs only to me." This alone was very flawed thinking on the part of Ivan. If asset protection were that easy, no legal industry would have grown up around asset protection. To Katerina, however, it seemed like a good idea. She went along with the plan and transferred her ownership of the house to Ivan "as his sole and separate property."

Even worse, Ivan did not take the next crucial step. He did not write a will in which he left everything including the house to his wife. How many people worry about such things at forty-eight? Because the house was in his name "as his sole and separate property," when he died, it was not considered "marital property" anymore, and guess what? Their children had an immediate legal right to part of the house. Of the four kids, three were adults, and one was still a minor. The complexities swiftly multiplied.

Katerina sat in my office, crying. "Not only have I lost my husband," she despaired, "but now I have this issue with my own house." She was not going to be able to sell the house without going through probate. She wasn't even going to be able to refinance it without going through probate. And she was certainly going to have to give up some ownership to the children.

Here, we have a clear case of how what you don't know you don't know can hurt you, and hurt you badly. Katerina's struggle could have been avoided if she and Ivan had consulted an estate planning attorney and put their affairs in order. With the right will and the right living trust, no probate hearing would have been required, and Katerina would have taken full control of the house.

Would that have cost a little money? Yes. Would it have been worth it? Oh, yes.

## PROBATE GETS EXPENSIVE *FAST*

Probate is not just a hassle and a potential nightmare, but it can be very expensive. Why? Never mind the court fees, which are annoying, but manageable for most. Probate gets expensive because the cases are rarely as simple as Bob Jr.'s, with a clear will and a single heir.

In most of the probate cases I see, heirs are not working their way through the court process on their own. They may have *started out* doing it themselves, but they quickly become frustrated, annoyed, and unhappy. So, they hire an attorney to finish the process for them. Typically, the executor of the will also takes a fee to complete his or her responsibilities. All this adds up quickly.

In California and New York, a million-dollar estate typically pays almost $50,000 in probate fees and expenses. Often, these fees are based on the gross value of the assets of the estate *without regard to debts.* Think about that. If the debts to the estate are high, it's easy to see how the whole process could end up under water.

## MINOR CHILDREN PRESENT A SPECIAL PROBLEM

The costs of probate will go up considerably if the succession involves orphaned minor children. But in that case, of course, more than money is at stake.

When children are under eighteen, and no parent survives, the state or other "interested person" will seek a guardianship for the child's "person" and a guardian for the child's money, or "estate." Sometimes, these will be the same person, and sometimes they will not. In the Introduction of this book, we discussed a common situation in which these two roles should be separated. Let's look at these issues more deeply.

In most states, if someone under the age of eighteen inherits any money of significance, the question of guardianship for this money will arise in court. If the child does not have a living parent, and a parent has not nominated anyone, the court will start looking for suitable guardians for both the person and the estate. If the child inherits a couple of hundred thousand dollars, the cost of creating these guardianships alone will cost $10,000 to $15,000. It's not uncommon for the full cost of a probate process that includes a guardianship court proceeding for minor orphans to run $100,000 in legal fees.

Why so much? For starters, the court generally appoints an investigator to look into the backgrounds of nominated guardians. There's typically an additional attorney appointed to represent the minor child. The costs of hiring these people is not paid for by the state if the estate has the ability to pay.

But minor children present an even greater risk to your financial legacy. The moment the child turns seventeen and 366 days, he or she can take complete control of their money and blow it, which they usually do. Do you remember being eighteen? As I mentioned in Part One, boys generally buy cars. Girls buy clothes or cars for their boyfriends. In any case, they have been thinking about this money for a long time—and now they've got it.

Guardianship creates a heavy responsibility whether it's guardianship of the person, of the finances, or of both. The guardian will have to file an accounting with the court every two years, or as the court may otherwise order, and give a final accounting when the child turns eighteen. If you don't find a suitable guardian to agree to take on this role before something happens to you, the court may not be able to find a good, willing guardian at all. And your children will end up in foster homes with strangers as their guardians.

Guardians sometimes drop out before the child comes of age, or they do something irresponsible, which makes it vital to move them out of the role. In that case, the court will appoint a new guardian.

Many other situations will trigger a guardianship or a con-servatorship (i.e., guardianship for an adult) proceeding. These include mentally incompetent, adult dependents and mentally incompetent, surviving spouses. Again, if you don't plan for these possibilities in advance, a court-appointed social worker will.

How do guardians get put into place? If you die suddenly, and your children under eighteen have no surviving parent (divorced or otherwise), social services may claim responsibility for them. The relevant agency will then start interacting with family members. "Did they find a will? Did the parent make some other nomination for a guardian? Did the deceased parent write anything down that says, 'I want this person to care for my minor child?'"

If no one petitions to become the guardian, social services will petition the court to name a guardian. If social services identify a nominated guardian, and the nominee agrees, then he or she must go on to file a petition with the court to become the guardian. No petition, no guardian. The pro-cess is not automatic.

The guardianship process and hearing are very much like the probate process I described for Bob Jr. A potential guardian has to file a stack of papers and appear in court. But in this case, he or she will also have to go through a pretty serious background check, including perhaps fingerprints, etc. As mentioned, this investigative process will indeed cost money, paid by the estate.

No nominee designated by the deceased parents? Social services will start sorting through the rest of your family. Any grandparents out there? What if four grandparents are alive, *and both sets want to be the guardians?* Now that can be a nasty fight.

Such situations cannot always be avoided. But their cost, their burden on the family, and the chance of a bad outcome can all be greatly reduced by proper estate planning. And all parents should do it.

I believe it is *every* parent's responsibility to create proper documents nominating guardians for minor children— every parent with any child under eighteen. In fact, just as important, I believe parents should create a living trust (see later in this chapter) and designate a trustee to watch over their children's financial estate until they are well *older* than eighteen—perhaps until they complete an undergraduate education or later.

### PROBATE IS DANGEROUSLY *PUBLIC*

Like Bob Jr., most people are shocked to learn that probate offers the family no privacy whatsoever. Literally, anyone can go to any court in America, walk up to the probate filing window, and say, "I'd like to see such and such file number." The clerk will turn over a file that will include the probate petition and lots of other documents containing the names and addresses of executors, beneficiaries, and anyone else involved, adults and minors alike. The date of the inheritance and the amount of the inheritance is a matter of public record, along with the specific value of all assets in the estate and all of its debts.

Right there, for anyone to see.

Any scam artist who wants to troll court records and take advantage of people who have just inherited money could do no better than start at the probate filing window. Creditors of a beneficiary may subscribe to a data service and say, "Hey, I'm owed $100,000 by Bob Jr. Tell me whenever his name pops up in court records. This same creditor may show up at the probate hearing and say, "Don't give the money to this heir, give it to me." I have seen it happen.

Conservatorship processes for adults offer limited privacy. If you get Alzheimer's disease, and have not made proper prior arrangements, your conservatorship hearing will become a matter of public record. The medical portion of your file can remain "sealed," but family ties and the amounts of money spent become a matter of public record. This means that all of your personal details, from the names of your relatives to a second degree of kinship to your financial records, will be available to anyone who inquires about them. If \$118.36 was spent for adult diapers at Walgreens three years ago, anyone can find out.

## ENTER THE LIVING TRUST

I have left out a lot of details about the actual processes of probate courts. Why? Because solid advice for navigating probate requires a whole other book, and an attorney.

This book has a different job. This book exists to keep heirs *out of probate court altogether*. Consider that statement your mission, whether you are planning your own succession or helping your parents plan theirs. Regardless of your financial situation, your goal should be to make your wishes *so clear* that no judge has to clarify them. Then, *structure your estate* so it can be passed on without a hearing.

How can you avoid the terrible hassle of probates and guardian processes? The arguments? The uncertainty? The delays?

*Do a good estate plan with its foundation in a living trust.*

### WHAT IS A LIVING TRUST, EXACTLY?

Much of the rest of this book will be about constructing a good living trust. But what *is* a living trust, exactly?

As I explained briefly earlier in the book, you can think of a living trust as a kind of vessel, a bucket which you create, and into which you place your stuff. Some things, like IRAs, 401(k)s, annuities and life insurance do not go into the trust, (See Mistake #5).

Basically, when your stuff goes into a bucket, it's a lot easier for you to carry around, a lot easier to track, and a whole lot easier to pass on to another person. Forgive me for extending the metaphor, but if your stuff is *not* in a bucket, when you die, it falls onto the ground. Then other people have to find it, figure out who owned it, and go to court to prove it's now theirs. Only then can they pick it up off the ground.

When you (or you and your spouse) create a living trust, you literally transfer many of the things you own into that trust. And while you are alive, you remain in control of that trust. When you die or become incapacitated, you give control of your trust to someone else. Because, according to law, the living trust *owns* all that stuff, and *the trust survives you,* no probate is required. There is nothing to prove to a judge. No *"probare"* needed. The trust continues to be the legal owner of the assets. Control of the trust simply passes to a new trustee.

As I also said in the Introduction, a living trust may sound like a legal fiction, but it is not. Living trusts are the very sensible way our society has devised to make succession easy, logical, and low cost. Trusts are the way we preserve legacies—a way of cheating some of the chaos created by death.

Every living trust includes at least three key roles. *And while you are alive and of sound mind, you can play all three roles in the trust.*

First, there's the *grantor.* That's the person (or jointly as a married couple) who creates the trust "bucket" and puts all their stuff into it. In the beginning, that would be you, or your parents, if you're helping them get this done. Sometimes, other names are used for the grantor, such as the settlor, trustor, or trust maker, but it's all the same idea. Attorneys prefer *grantor*, because that word has a specific meaning in our tax laws—the Internal Revenue Code.

Second, there's the *trustee.* That's the person (or couple) who controls the trust. Again, while the grantor is alive and well, that's usually you.

Third, there's the *beneficiary.* This is the person (or couple) who has a right to *all* the benefit of the stuff in the bucket. While you are alive, this is definitely you.

Again, when you are alive and well, you generally play all three roles—that's why it's a *living* trust, because the trust protects you now, and continues to protect your estate when you are no longer able to protect it yourself. All your stuff is in the bucket, and as the grantor, when you get more stuff, you just add it to the bucket.

Need to pay your credit card bill? Your mortgage? Get some groceries? Buy a ticket to Hawaii? As trustee, you are the only one who can reach into the bucket and take stuff out for use by the beneficiary. You can do that as often as you like, because while you are alive, *you are also the beneficiary*.

Your kids go off to college? You write a check from the trust.

Your daughter gets married? Paid from the trust.

You can treat the money in a trust completely as *your own* money, the house owned by the trust as *your* house, the car in the trust as *your* car—though again, in the eyes of the law, it all technically *belongs* to the trust.

### HOW A LIVING TRUST PROTECTS YOU AND YOUR ESTATE

Now, what if you become so sick that you cannot exercise proper control over your assets? Without a trust, a lot of uncertainty and confusion attends disability. (See Mistake #8: Forgetting to Plan for Disability.)

With a trust, everyone knows exactly what will happen. Why? *Because it's written down.* You will have designated someone else to take the role of *trustee* in your absence. Crucially, however, because you (or you and your spouse) remain the sole *beneficiaries* of the trust, the new trustee can *only* use your assets to take care of *your* needs: food, clothing, and mortgage payments, for example. In the event that you become capable of taking the trustee role again, the trust returns that power to you.

Here's the key to avoiding probate: when you (or you and your spouse) pass away, the trust continues. It does not die with you. Only the names playing the roles change. There's a new trustee and a new beneficiary, specified by you in the trust. And, presto! Your assets can be dealt with and passed on without any court or probate process required.

If Bob Sr. had created a living trust, placed all of his assets and accounts into that trust, and then named Bob Jr. as trustee when he died, well, our story would have had a very different ending.

On that first Monday morning when Bob Jr. showed up at Friendly Bank, he would only have needed to bring a copy of the signed trust, his father's death certificate, and his photo ID. That's it. The bank would have immediately given him control of his father's accounts. Bob Jr. may also have had to get a "Taxpayer Identification Number (TIN)" from the IRS by submitting a form SS-4. The TIN belongs to the trust and functions like a Social Security number for the trust to deal with assets in the trust. Bob Jr. would not use his Social Security number, or that of his late father.

The manager would have said, "Terrific. You are now the trustee. You are in charge. We will change the name on the living trust account here at Friendly Bank, and starting today, you can sign the checks."

That's how simple the succession would have been. No published notices, no court dates, no legal fees, no judge, and no "form pleading." Just an orderly passage of assets, generation to generation, in exactly the manner Bob Sr. would have desired.

Had minor children been involved, Bob Sr. could have designated a trustee to watch over the assets in his trust until those children were out of college. And in separate documents, as part of a complete estate plan, he could have nominated proper guardians for their well-being. In doing this, of course, Bob Sr. would have used an attorney, because a trusteeship for a minor is a complex undertaking in which the trustee will accept unlimited personal liability for all acts and omissions.

There's more, of course. If Bob Sr. were a partner in a business, he could have used his estate plan to designate a trustee to take over his decision-making powers and business assets for the benefit of his estate and heirs. Maybe that trustee would have been Bob Jr. Or perhaps, it would have been a business associate he trusted, with Bob Jr. still being the beneficiary.

I hope you now understand why you must do whatever you can to protect your heirs from probate—and how a living trust will be critical to your plans.

Even with this understanding, however, it is imperative that you avoid making the mistake of assuming that all living trusts are more or less the same. Or, that they can be created with some cut-and-paste template.

In Mistake #9, we'll look at the different kinds of living trusts, and how they must be *custom-built* for the complexities of modern families and modern life.

# ASSUMING ALL TRUSTS ARE THE SAME

---

If you read through Mistake #10, you now understand how a mere "last will and testament" does not provide the vital mechanisms offered by a living trust. A will can be partly disregarded by a judge or indefinitely delayed by probate. A living trust offers you the chance to bypass many of the frustrations of the probate, conservatorship, and guardianship systems.

Do not, however, be tempted create a living trust by yourself, or on the cheap. I urge you to reread the Introduction before you run to the internet and download a generic living trust template, or pay $59.99 for a "Guaranteed 100 Percent Legal Online Living Trust in One Hour or Less." If my warnings about gathering a "mushroom stew for your children" still fail to convince you to hire a qualified estate attorney, I urge you to consider the message of this chapter: there is no such thing as a generic trust.

A single person needs one kind of trust and a married couple needs another. Depending on their circumstances, a married couple may want to create a joint trust or two single trusts.

Sometimes a married couple should opt for an "A-B trust" or even an "A-B-C trust." These trusts have become obsolete for most purposes (see Mistake #4) but may be highly relevant to blended families for a variety of reasons, including limiting the surviving spouse's control over the deceased spouse's share of the estate. In this way, an A-B trust protects the deceased spouse's beneficiaries from the whims of the surviving spouse. Upon the death of the first spouse, an A-B or A-B-C trust sub-divides into an A trust (also known as a "Survivor's Trust") and a B trust (also known as an "Exemption Trust," a "Bypass Trust," or a "Family Trust" with separate control mechanisms). A "C trust" is like a B Trust but has different capital gains and death tax rules.

Sometimes, it's appropriate to create a "revocable" trust and sometimes an "irrevocable" trust. As the word implies, an irrevocable trust cannot be amended or revoked. Generally speaking, an irrevocable trust serves the purpose of preventing property from being included in your total assets—your estate—during life or after death, or both. Some clients who are helping elderly parents get financial help for healthcare will use an irrevocable trust as part of the overall estate plan. It often provides the best protection of assets from creditors and predators, as the assets have "irrevocably" changed ownership.

Many useful trusts are not "living trusts" at all. The term "living trust" is short for "*inter-vivos* trust" or "a trust between living people." Importantly, a living trust does not require a separate taxpayer identification number while you are alive, and you need not file a separate tax return for your living trust. But, as you will see in some of the upcoming chapters, it's not the right vehicle for all situations. For example, living trusts are "revocable."

Many problems arise from what we attorneys call an "I Love You Trust," in which somebody creates a document which says, in essence, "I love you. I'm going to give you everything I have when I die," without any consideration of the taxes or legal pitfalls the loved one will face. You should not assume, however, that a well-written trust will include all the tax-planning provisions within its own structure. In 2014, 2017, and again in 2019, we saw a significant change in tax law, which made it foolish to include certain then-common tax planning provisions in living trusts.

IRAs pose a special problem; you may want to consider an

IRA Legacy Trust—which became more relevant than ever under new tax laws. In fact, whatever else you skip in this book, don't skip Mistake #5: Assuming Your Living Trust Covers Things Like IRAs, 401(k)s, 403(b)s, 457s, Annuities, and Insurance.

Bottom line: you have to know what you are doing.

Take a couple with a large estate, say $5 million, $10 million, or more. The trust and will can be structured so that all the property goes to the surviving spouse. That sounds great. But suppose the husband dies and now *all* the assets are in the wife's estate. If the assets continue to grow, they can become larger than the inheritance tax exemption the wife has at her death. As of this writing, the individual federal, tax-free limit for estates is over $11 million—but will go down to $6 million or so on January 1, 2026. The $6M number is indexed to inflation. If her assets grew beyond that point (quite possible), the estate could take a huge tax hit. A married couple doubles up on the exemption, but when one spouse dies, the survivor must file a Form 706 and elect "portability." This process should be handled with qualified professionals.

A tax-savvy estate attorney will know the trust strategies that protect the estate from such dangers. For example, some of the deceased's assets could be held in a separate *irrevocable trust* created at his death. If properly structured, such assets might not be counted in the wife's estate, so the total could grow to an unlimited amount and still not trigger the inheritance tax.

Other "tax planning trusts" might include charitable trusts, which are creatures of specific tax statutes. In a charitable trust, some of the assets of the trust go to a charity and the other part of the assets go to you or your loved ones. We'll learn more in Mistake #4.

Here's a further example of a non-generic trust. Suppose you are middle-class, but you have a wealthy child. When you die, you may not want to give that child your property outright, because when *the child dies,* the grandchildren will have to pay death taxes. A good estate attorney can create a separate trust to be used for the benefit of your child when you die, but has been excluded from your child's own estate. The wealthy child can enjoy full access to the money during his or her lifetime, but this "generation skipping" trust preserves the wealth for the grandkids—even though it does not actually skip any generations at all.

## TRUSTS TO PROTECT AGAINST LAWSUITS, CREDITORS, PREDATORS, AND DIVORCE

Any significant asset can be threatened by creditors, predators, and major relationship shifts like divorce. We lawyers know that a single lawsuit can completely wipe out an inheritance. A good trust will take into account the highly specific dangers faced by your circumstances—both during your life, and when you've passed that asset on to your heirs.

Suppose you own an apartment building and you have hired somebody to manage it. When you die, you pass the apartment building on to your child, outright.

One day, long after you are gone, the apartment manager says something stupid to a prospective tenant like, "We don't rent to people like you." (Feel free to insert any protected class for the word "people.") The prospective tenant sues your child, even though he or she never hired the manager, and like you, never instructed the idiot to say any such thing. If the lawsuit is based on race, disability, or similar protected circumstances, then your child will probably not be covered by insurance. That lawsuit can take not only the apartment building, but potentially all your child's *other* assets as well.

I could come up with any number of similar examples where people do things that are not your family's fault but trigger legal responsibility.

A savvy estate attorney can structure a series of trusts so when you die, instead of your child inheriting the apartment building outright, it goes from your bucket into a second bucket. Your child did not create that second bucket—you were the grantor of the asset in that bucket, and you are gone. Your child can now control and benefit from the apartment building, but he or she can be personally shielded from the threats of creditors, predators, and lawsuits. This same strategy can ensure that your child does not lose such assets in a divorce. Again, because your child does not technically own the asset, it is owned by an irrevocable trust "bucket."

We'll learn more about predators, creditors, and divorce in Mistake #6: Letting Third Parties Take Advantage of Your Beneficiaries.

In the ever-expanding universe of trusts, you will find trusts which pour from one bucket to the next, trusts within trusts, and many kinds of children's trusts. Each must be carefully coordinated with your overall estate plan. And just to repeat, none are "generic."

## HELPING MINORS AND UNTRUSTWORTHY HEIRS

You can, for example, set up a trust for the benefit of your children into which other relatives can place money. Suppose both sets of grandparents are interested in using their annual gift-tax exemption to help their grandkids save for college. Such a trust would not technically be considered a "living trust," but could go a long way toward funding your children's education.

Even a basic living trust to benefit your children must be carefully considered from every angle. For example, as I have discussed (see Mistake #10), you may not want your living trust to read simply: "When the kid is eighteen, he gets it all."

Or, even when he's twenty-five. You may sit down with your estate attorney and say, "Gee, my kid is twenty-five and still lives at home. He sits on the couch all day smoking dope and playing video games. Already this drives me crazy. At least, if I die tomorrow, I don't want to go on supporting that lifestyle. Maybe I could just give him a little bit each year, but not quite enough to live on, so he'll have to go out and get a job?"

With a properly written living trust, controlled by a separate trustee, you can indeed make that specific kind of provision to help your child move forward after you are gone. But you cannot download a template from the internet and make that kind of provision. You can't fill out an online form, which will make that work.

## HOW TO GET A PERSONALIZED TRUST

Now that you realize how a *personalized* living trust, along with other kinds of trusts require some serious expertise, how do you go about finding that expertise? In the Introduction, I explained some *tells* for identifying a good estate attorney. But the best attorneys don't just learn by doing estate planning. Before anyone can create a really workable and airtight plan, he or she must thoroughly understand what happens *after* that plan is triggered.

When my firm trains lawyers in estate planning, we don't start by teaching them how to meet with clients and draw up trusts. We start by teaching them about the probate process, the conservatorship process (see Mistake #8), and trust administration. We get them directly involved in the events which *follow* the death of a client. That way, they see how the crucial decisions made during planning play out in the real world.

Lights go on for these lawyers: "Gee, if this couple had just added a provision for care of Uncle Ted to their living trust, all this hassle for their heirs could have been avoided." Or, "I wish someone had told these people not to name these particular two people as co-trustees. As a result, this brother and sister have really come to hate each other." Or, just as commonly, "Gee, if this couple had come back every five or six years and reviewed their estate plan, everything would be working a heck of a lot better. So much changed in the thirty years before they died that it's now impossible to administer this trust the way they intended!"

Unfortunately, many attorneys do not get this kind of training. They just don't have the experience of babysitting multiple estates through probate, setting up conservatorships, or administering trusts. They haven't litigated wills on behalf of heirs. They don't see how different kinds of trusts lead to different kinds of results. So, just like their clients, attorneys all too often assume that a "standard living trust" will be good enough.

Once you've found that good attorney, the one who has actually walked through probate and *administered* trusts and conservatorships—your next job is to make sure they sit down with you to ask a lot of questions. Make sure they turn over every rock and force you to face whatever the two of you find underneath.

Tough questions may include the unexpected, like: "Do you get along with your siblings?"

Why would such a question matter? Because if you are incapacitated, *a sibling could easily step in and cause havoc in your planning,* even if you haven't spoken in thirty years, and even if you have adult children. It happens.

Based on your individual circumstances, an attorney should also ask questions like, "Do you get along with your spouse? With your ex-spouse? Will your children get along when they sit in the room hearing the will read? Is your son or daughter likely to face divorce some day? Does he or she have a complex tax situation? If you become incapacitated, what will happen to that vote you have on the board of your brother-in-law's business?"

You can see more examples of good question-asking by attorneys in the Introduction.

## PARALEGALS AREN'T ENOUGH

Your attorney has to dig deep.

As I have now complained many times, attorneys often do not bother to dig deeply. They may simply pull up the John and Judy Smith Living Trust they did last week and replace all the names with Fred and Sally Jones.

But "search-and-replace planning" gets even worse with paralegals. Even if I have convinced you not to download a template or log into a "living trust service," I worry that you may still attempt to save money by avoiding the services of an attorney. You may think, "Okay, but I have a very simple situation. I'll save money on lawyers by going to a paralegal to get an estate plan drawn up."

Paralegals have been trained in a variety of common legal processes. They do great work in many realms, and they are invaluable to keeping my own practice on track. But with all due respect to the profession, you must recognize the limits of a paralegal's scope. Not only do paralegals lack the training and experience of a lawyer, they simply do not *think* like lawyers.

Law school not only teaches people legalities and case law, it truly rewires people's brains. I will not dwell on this rewiring process, as much has been written about it by others. But I know it occurs, perhaps as an actual change in brain chemistry.

Lawyers learn to think ahead to many more moves of the chess game. They anticipate objections to documents. They anticipate the emotions of judges and litigants. When reading, they read between the lines. When speaking, they watch body language.

Let me give you a quick analogy from the medical world. I had a colleague who developed intestinal cancer go in to discuss his surgery. The surgeon says, "You know, before we do surgery, I want you to meet with your cardiologist for one more checkup. Don't worry, it's routine." The cardiologist gets out his stethoscope and listens to the pulse on my colleague's neck, and immediately orders a raft of tests. Bottom line: the guy has a hunk of fat nearly blocking his neck artery. The cardiologist immediately arranges for this to be removed. Later, the cardiologist tells my friend that had he not come to see the cardiologist and had gone through with the abdominal surgery with the blockage in his neck, he would have died. Indeed, *if he was lucky, he would have died*. Most likely, he would have had a massive stroke.

When you have surgery, you go to experts in the medical field. These professionals look for the unexpected and the unanticipated. They see *clues only experience will notice.* My colleague went in about one problem, but the pros saw something more.

It's the job of an expert living trust lawyer to identify "fact patterns" the layman does not see and follow through based on experience. We expert lawyers have been trained to look at common fact patterns and possible results, then apply them to new situations—to see around corners, and to make sure you deal with "what you don't know you don't know." (See Introduction.)

You really do need someone "to think like a lawyer" and anticipate the consequences of a plan that will play out for decades after you are gone.

## THE PROCESS FOR A CUSTOM PLAN

In my firm, we follow a highly defined process to make sure we've turned over every stone, followed up on every clue, leveraged our "lawyerly thinking," and crafted the best possible estate plan for our clients. Our process happens to have ten steps. Your attorney may follow seven or fifteen steps. But make sure those steps can be fully articulated. If not, look elsewhere.

Here's a quick summary of our approach:

1. Education of the client, starting with a seminar or book.
2. Detailed diagnostics: Who are you? Who belongs to you? What are your assets?
3. First attorney meeting.
4. Review of all data by a senior paralegal.
5. Input of data to professional software.
6. Review of software inputs by a second attorney.
7. Creation of draft documents by the software.
8. Client receives and reviews documents.
9. Client signs documents.
10. Continuing client education and regular plan reviews.

### STEP 1: CLIENT EDUCATION MATTERS...A LOT

In Step 1, we want to make sure that the client gets a basic education in the issues and processes of estate planning. We don't want anyone to come in and sit blankly in front of an all-knowing lawyer whose whole demeanor says, in essence, "be quiet and listen to me." That kind of relationship might be fine in some legal work, but not in estate planning, which requires a true give-and-take. No lawyer can possibly know all the issues pertaining to your individual circumstances, so *you are going to have to become educated enough to have a proper discussion.* And you are going to have to trust him or her enough to discuss some of the most difficult areas of your family life.

Like many firms, we educate our clients with a seminar. Increasingly, following the impact of COVID-19, these are happening virtually over the internet. Other firms will host radio shows, produce webinars, or write books like this one. But a good estate firm is always educating, educating, educating.

## EARNED EXPERTISE VS. STRONG OPINION

Respected author and blogger, Seth Godin, calls earned expertise the "I've Dealt with This Before" difference.

He wrote: "...[t]here's a huge gulf between earned expertise and strong opinion. Knowing what others who have come before have done...is demonstrably more effective than simply acting as if your opinion matters. Whether you're dealing [with] a lawsuit [or I might add, a living trust]... you're better off talking with someone who has earned their experience. There's a reason that there are very few loud amateur locksmiths. Either the lock opens or it doesn't. Untrained voices tend to reserve their work for endeavors in which the results are either difficult to measure or happen far in the future."

It is very hard for you, a "normal" person (as opposed to an expert living trust lawyer), to measure the effectiveness of a living trust. It's doubly difficult because a living trust won't be used until far into the future following your incapacity or death.

In this way, a client comes in empowered, not just with an understanding of the process, but with knowledge of how to identify personal issues and questions. The longer the list you develop, the better. Who will make medical decisions for you if you get sick? Who's going to be in charge of your money? Who's going to be in charge of your kids? Your disabled dependents? Who will handle your trust administration? The more advance work you do, the better you will use your attorney's time, and the more tailored planning he or she will be able to do on your behalf.

## STEP 2: GETTING *ALL* THE DETAILS

In Step 2, after educating the client and identifying key issues, our office performs a detailed "diagnostic." When you go to a doctor's office, the staff will ask what medications and vitamins you are taking. They'll check your temperature and blood pressure. They'll run some blood tests. In our office, we set out to understand your family structure, your asset structure, and of course, your hopes and dreams for the legacy you wish to leave for the next generation.

I should note that the diagnostic process is more extensive for people with very large and complex estates—over, say, $10 million in assets. In such cases, we often need a number of extra discovery steps before we can move to serious planning.

In any case, we really do need all the details! At the end of this book, you will find a checklist to prepare for your estate planning meeting. Putting all this information together, as well as doing some advance thinking about the issues, will go a long way toward making the process smooth, complete, and smart.

## STEP 3: THE FIRST ATTORNEY MEETING

That first sit-down meeting in the estate planning process often proves crucial. I always insist that an experienced attorney, not a paralegal or support staff, handles the initial, in-depth discussion. An attorney "thinking like a lawyer" will immediately see issues that might otherwise get lost down the line.

The older I get, the longer my first meetings tend to run. I admit that when I was first starting out as an estate planning attorney, first meetings might last just twenty minutes. That was when I didn't know what I didn't know.

My goal in that first sit-down is often to identify any "pain points." Usually, these are not just financial, but personal. The pain points can be highly emotional: estranged children, angry ex-spouses, troubled businesses. Difficult, but vital to discuss.

Earlier, I spoke about a twenty-five-year-old still at home, playing video games and smoking dope. But often it's far worse. A client will say, "I've really been struggling. My daughter has an addiction, and it's destroying her life. Right now, if I were not supporting her, she might be living on the street. I don't know how to deal with this. I lie awake at night, and I think, *'My God, if something happens to me, what's going to happen to my child? What if she gets too much money? Would that kill her? What will her brother and sister do?'*"

Or a man might say, "We don't have enough money. If something happens to my spouse, I can't live on one salary. What can we do about that?" Or, "I'm worried that the stock market will crash. We're retired and everything is invested. What if we outlive our money?"

Some of these issues may seem outside the scope of estate planning, but we try to include every issue—often with the help of allied professionals. Clients must feel comfortable bringing all their "stuff" to the table at that first meeting. No guilt, no blame: we just look each question straight in the eye.

## STEPS 4–8: CREATING THE DOCUMENTS

After I have all the data and have unearthed all the issues in Step 3, I will have an internal meeting with our senior paralegal in Step 4.

No doubt, I did not say enough good things about paralegals earlier. I will tell you, as a lawyer, those meetings often offer me a heavy dose of humility. A good paralegal will make sure every single data point has been covered, all the questions answered, all the proper diagnostics run, all the account numbers discovered, all the investment vehicles identified, and all the client properties recorded. We sit down and go over everything. I use my "lawyer brain" to ferret out issues, and the paralegal uses their "paralegal brain" to double-check the dotting of the i's and the crossing of the t's.

In Step 5, we leverage the technology, which will do the initial assembly of all the documents for a complete estate plan. The software requires extensive data input. A specialized, attorney-level package will ask us far more than the fifty or so questions in an online trust-creation algorithm. It will require 400 to 500 responses, leading to highly customized drafts. This process is not a substitute for human judgment, but a tremendous aid to human brainpower and efficiency. As I noted in the Introduction, such software now leads to highly tailored and customized estate plans and saves our clients tens of thousands of dollars over manual processes.

Since neither I nor the paralegal is perfect, in Step 6, we assign a qualified attorney to the task of reviewing the software inputs.

Only then does the software do its thing and create the draft documents, which are sent for client review, along with highlights on key issues. Attached notes might read, "Is this exactly what you meant regarding that property?"

I'm compressing the steps, but I hope you understand the value of a defined process with multiple checkpoints and attorney reviews before anything gets to you for your review.

One word of caution: don't assume that *every* word in a legal document is customizable. There are certain paragraphs that a lawyer will not modify. These include the powers of the trustee, definitions, etc. These are equivalent to computer coding. Some clients will want to get into the weeds and change highly technical language. These parts of the trust are necessary to the proper functioning of the trust and not for the individual client to customize. I would never tell a surgeon how to conduct a surgery, because it would put my health in jeopardy. Likewise, tinkering with the legal technical terms may cause big problems for your loved ones down the road.

### STEP 9: ACTUALLY SIGNING THE DOCUMENTS!

Throughout this book, you will hear me emphasize the all-too-common situations in which people simply do not get around to signing documents they have had prepared, be they trusts, transfers of property to trusts, powers of attorney—you name it. Whether the issue is hesitation or procrastination, the results can be disastrous.

## THAT IMPORTANT STEP 10

After an estate plan is signed, Step 10 includes continuing client education, followed by regular estate plan reviews and updates, which are best done at least every three years or as your situation changes. Changes include a birth, death, divorce, retirement, moving to a new state, changing jobs, etc.

As discussed in the Introduction, a modern attorney with a significant estate practice will include such reviews at no additional charge. In my firm, we believe free reviews to be an ethical obligation. If your attorney wants your plan to be successful, he or she must create no barrier to you picking up the phone with a question, or scheduling an appointment for a fresh look. Your attorney may, however, reasonably charge something for a rewrite of the plan.

Never skip a review. After reading the above, I hope you no longer believe in a "generic trust." And I hope you no longer see any substitute to working through your issues with an experienced attorney. But please recognize that even the best attorney cannot write an estate plan that will stay relevant no matter how your issues change.

We will learn more about updates when we've counted

down to Mistake #2: Forgetting to Keep Up with Changes. For now, let's move on to a terrible mistake indeed—betting that you will never get seriously ill.

# FORGETTING TO PLAN FOR DISABILITY

———

Forgive me, but I need to start this chapter with a statement that's both brutal and true:

*A disability is often harder on a family than a death.*

Why? Because if you become seriously disabled, your loved ones will have to deal with many of the same legal issues as when you die, but they will also have to take care of you. A serious disability is not just difficult and draining for everyone, but shockingly expensive. A nursing home runs from $3,000 on up to $30,000 or more a month, depending on quality and level of care. In-home help can be just as expensive. Both Medicare and health insurance stop paying for institutional daily care after a short time limit. And most government aid programs expect you to exhaust nearly all your assets before they step in to help.

A mental incapacity triggers the most significant consequences of all.

My wife and I learned this very personally.

Before my mother-in-law passed away in the spring of 2020, she suffered from Alzheimer's disease, and my wife was her primary caregiver. She could provide little or no care for herself. As Nancy Reagan said, it's a "long, long goodbye."

My mother-in-law was once a strong woman who raised four boys and a daughter. This made the emotional burden on my wife that much harder as their roles reversed. My wife became the parent, and the parent became the child. Because I have pledged myself to honesty in this book, I will say this aloud: my wife's mother became a 102-pound two-year-old. I do not say this to be heartless, it was just true.

Fun activities ceased, conversation became limited—but they still enjoyed each other's company. Importantly and tragically, because my in-laws never bought a good long term care policy (a big mistake), the cost factors demanded that my wife provide the daily personal care—leaving little time for their positive moments.

## MORE CHALLENGING THAN DEATH

From the standpoint of legal and family logistics, mental incapacity often proves more challenging than death. That's because while death is a clearly defined state, incapacity is not. To quote Yogi Berra, "It ain't over till it's over." From a legal perspective, incapacity creates a twilight zone of uncertainty, which often causes strife within families, drains estates, and leads to unnecessary and debilitating court battles.

In the Introduction, I noted that 80 percent of Americans will face a period of sustained disability before their deaths. Most of those Americans will not have done even the most rudimentary planning for this event. A "last will and testament" does not adequately provide for the succession of an estate; *it does nothing to provide for mental incapacity, because it's not legally effective until death.*

Remember that in your decline, someone *will* have to take action. If your mental agility fades, you may become a threat to yourself or other people. You may become substantially unable to resist fraud, duress, menace from predators, or the undue influence of others. If you become unable to provide for your own food, clothing, hygiene, and shelter, someone else must be given the responsibility for your person. Someone else must decide where you will live and with whom you will associate.

## WHAT IF I HAVE NO PLAN?

If you enter a period of mental incapacity due to a stroke, dementia, Alzheimer's, or other causes, there may come a point when you really should not be in control of your bank account or other affairs. At this point, if your family doesn't step in, the government will.

If someone notices that you have started writing checks for $5,000 to the pizza delivery guy, and no family member *with legal authority* steps in, the county in which you reside *will* enter your home and take over. Certain institutions, like banks, hospitals, and senior centers are on the watch for moments like this, and they are required to report their suspicions about your mental capacity to law enforcement. They are called "mandated reporters."

Typically, a county social services agency will be asked to take action. And often, social services will call in a special law enforcement unit called Adult Protective Services. The actions of Adult Protective Services are not public. You cannot get access to their reports, and you cannot find out what all these people have been saying about you—so unlike a criminal, you cannot "confront your accuser."

At that crucial moment, if you have created the proper documents to give someone a "durable power of attorney for property" in case of your incapacity, along with a "durable power of attorney for healthcare," or an "advanced healthcare directive," someone you have previously designated can step in and take control from the county. Importantly, this agent working on your behalf can prevent action by a court to create a "conservatorship" for you. As we will see, a conservatorship represents a serious loss of rights.

Of course, your incapacity may happen much faster, and be more serious than writing questionable checks.

## JACK CAUSES A CRISIS

Let's say Jack, who has been widowed for many years, has a major stroke at age seventy-four. Now he's lying unconscious in a Pasadena, California hospital. He was on the golf course, getting ready for a putt on the third green, and just collapsed. The doctors say that Jack may or may not recover from his stroke. In any case, he will definitely need daily physical care for years and will not be able to handle his own affairs.

Jack has two children, Charles and Mary, who live on opposite sides of the country. He also has a sister in East Sacramento, California, named Eleanor. She's seventy. All these folks have always gotten along, but over the years, they've kind of fallen out of touch.

Jack owns a house with some equity, but everyone figures he's still making mortgage and insurance payments. He has multiple bank accounts and investments, but no one's quite sure where they are. His red Porsche 911 still sits on the lot at the golf course. That's about as much as anyone knows. After all, Jack was only seventy-four, and until today, he was competently handling all of his own affairs.

Now Charles and Mary, who are both in their late forties, with careers and kids, have flown in to stand at Jack's bedside. Eleanor and her husband have shown up too. Charles has already been over to the house, and he found that Jack did make a simple will using an online service in which he divided everything nicely between Charles and Mary, with Mary as executor. But Jack never created the essential documents you will learn about later in this chapter. He never created a living trust. And he never designated powers of attorney for property or healthcare decisions.

Plus, well, he's still alive. So, now what?

If Jack had died, Mary would have taken over as executor, and after the funeral, she would have gone to probate court to get the will certified. She'd have struggled through the painful process we described for Bob Jr. in Mistake #10, but she would have figured out how to sell the house, settle Jack's debts, and divide what remained between herself and Charles.

Now, however, all has become uncertain. Of the people

standing next to the hospital bed, who will take control of the situation? And what about those not standing next to the bed, who may *want* to become involved? Many decisions will need to be made, and quickly.

The hospital (about $10,000 per day minimum and paid by Medicare) plans to discharge Jack to a rehabilitation center ($900 per day and paid by Medicare) that same afternoon. After that, Medicare *may* pay *part* of his care up to one-hundred days per calendar year. Or maybe not. It depends.

However, if Jack stops physical therapy, occupational therapy, or "plateaus" while in rehab, *Medicare stops paying*. Then, because he has no long-term care insurance, *he's on his own*. He's looking at $3,000 to $30,000 or more per month depending on where Jack lives and the level of care required. Jack, or his family, will pay for this care out of pocket. And if there's no room in Pasadena, he may get shipped out to a facility in Palm Springs, California.

Since he's not able to make his own decisions anymore, Jack's on someone else's watch.

*But whose?*

Jack's sister, Eleanor, steps up to say she knows about a really excellent care facility not far from Jack's home. It costs only about $10,500 a month, and a friend said Jack would love it. Eleanor also takes that moment to mention that Jack still owes her $20,000, which she says he borrowed from her five years ago. She tearfully recalls how she and Jack made a childhood pact to take care of each other if anything happened. Her husband puts his arm around her in support.

Jack's daughter, Mary, points out that she was the one named as executor in the will, so no doubt her father would like her to take responsibility now. She also strongly believes that the disabled are best cared for by those who love them, and not in a facility. She says she's more than willing to have Jack moved to her home, where she can take over his care with the help of some visiting staff. Of course, even the short trip from Pasadena, California, to her home in Westlake Village, California, would cost a considerable amount of money. She thinks she'll also need about $35,000 from Jack's estate to expand her guest room and add a bathroom he can use while in her care.

Her brother, Charles, gets a little annoyed with both of them. After all, his father may recover any day. Can't they just wait until the one-hundred days (or less) are up in skilled nursing to make any decisions? And anyway, all these options are expensive. Can Jack's estate even pay for it? How can they know, since none of them have any idea what's in his bank account? Will the house have to get sold? What if he wakes up and his house is gone? Also, right now, the hospital wants someone to sign off on the discharge plan. And by the way, the golf course would like to see the car removed from its parking lot.

Charles would love to help, but he has a job in Auburn, California, he needs to get back to right away.

## FRUSTRATIONS LEAD TO CONFLICT

The next day, both Mary and Eleanor call some banks and are surprised to discover that *neither of them* has the right to access Jack's accounts without going through an emergency court process. As the arguments escalate, it becomes likely that *both* Mary and Eleanor will petition the court to become Jack's conservator (more about the meaning of that term in a moment) and get access to his accounts.

Soon, all three of Jack's closest family members grow to dislike each other. Mary gets mad at Charles for being unhelpful, and she starts thinking she deserves more than 33 percent of any will. In probate court, which is the court that handles Conservatorships and guardianships as well as probate issues after a death. Eleanor again mentions getting reimbursed for her undocumented $20,000 loan.

But there's more.

As Jack's financial records come to light in court, they will become a matter of public record, along with all his debts. All the *other* relatives within a second degree of kinship will have to be notified—including the children of both Charles and Mary, some of whom are old enough to care what happens to grandpa and his money.

Both Eleanor and Mary have assigned themselves as conservators, but neither understands quite what she is asking for. Whoever becomes conservator will shoulder a considerable burden, and thanks to the ill will created during a court proceeding, she may be under continuous scrutiny from the others. She will have to provide an accounting to the court, down to the penny, every two years. This will include submitting a ledger with everything in and everything out; the growth or decline of investments. The works.

Meanwhile, Jack's care will begin eating up his estate. Whoever takes charge will have to make tough decisions, possibly resented by the others, about selling or renting the house and liquidating investments. The legal process itself will likely consume thousands, if not hundreds of thousands of dollars—depending on the value of the assets and the length of the fight. The same attorneys who practice probate law practice conservatorship (or guardianship) law, and they do not come cheap. Attorney fees in Los Angeles County, for example, can range from $500 to more than $800 per hour.

In the event that none of the three closest relatives applies to be conservator (or is approved by the court), then the county judge will appoint a "neutral" party—either a private professional fiduciary or the "public guardian" to take control. The public guardian's office is typically a county agency that looks out for the indigent. As it happens, the "indigent" sometimes have money but are poor in family. Or poor in family that cares.

## AVOIDING A CONSERVATORSHIP

Since incapacity before death is an 80 percent probability, you should plan for it. And you should plan to avoid a conservatorship if at all possible.

A conservator, sometimes called a "guardian," will have much more power than someone with "power of attorney." Once a conservator or guardian has been appointed over you by a court, you lose your liberty, along with considerable rights over your life. Someone else will tell you where to live, who to visit, and when. You won't vote anymore. If you are a gun owner, they'll take away your guns, too.

Once a conservator has been named, he or she will have the power to ask the court to confine you to an institution against your will. They will have the power to make all medical and financial decisions for you, and *you will lose the power to make these decisions for yourself* and take full control of your affairs.

You may have no input on who is named conservator by a court. Why? Because you will have been found incompetent to make such decisions.

It's likely that one of Jack's relatives will be appointed conservator, but Jack could have prevented much of this family strife, hassle, and expense simply by hiring an attorney to create a proper estate plan which took into account *the very high probably we all face of incapacity.*

If he trusted Mary, he could have named her as trustee for his living trust in case of his incapacity (see below). As trustee, she would have had immediate access to his accounts and his investments. Whether or not her decision to take him to her home in Westlake Village proved best in the long run or not, the decision would have been made without lawyers, legal expenses, or bitter court proceedings.

Which means there might have been enough money left over to do it right. Plus, everyone might still be getting along.

With a proper estate plan that takes into account disability, people don't have to argue about who is in charge, and the person in charge has the power to take the necessary and immediate actions.

Let's look at all the documents you need to put together with your attorney to plan ahead.

## EVERYONE SHOULD CONSIDER THESE ESSENTIAL DOCUMENTS

Earlier in the book we outlined the basic documents that make up an estate plan. Please flip back to the Introduction for the detailed summaries.

*You need every one of these documents in place, not just at the time of your death, but during any disability.*

As I said before, every adult over the age of eighteen should consider at least the first three documents below signed and available at all times. Any adult with assets, and certainly any adult with children, should consider making *all* the documents available and keeping them updated throughout their lives. At a minimum, these documents include:

- Durable Power of Attorney for Property
- Advance Healthcare Directive (Power of Attorney for Healthcare)
- HIPAA Authorization
- Living Will

- Living Trust
- "Pour-Over" Will

As you have seen in the case of Jack and his family, the failure to create all of these documents added considerable confusion, strife, and expense to an already-difficult health situation. It also led to an unnecessary legal process and the loss of his rights through a conservatorship.

Let's see how these documents function during a disability.

## GRANTING DURABLE POWER OF ATTORNEY AND NOMINATING A CONSERVATOR

Please do not be confused by the term "power of attorney." Many clients believe this term has something to do with the lawyer preparing their estate plan. Clients sometimes mistakenly fear that they are giving over some kind of power to their lawyer to make decisions for them. This is not true.

When you grant "durable power of attorney" to another person—any other person—you are designating that person as your *agent,* to act on your behalf. This may be your spouse, your child, a friend, or anyone, as long as he or she is an adult (eighteen or older) and not under a conservatorship or incarcerated. Now and then, someone may indeed choose an attorney for their agent, which adds confusion to the term.

"Durable" means "continuing even when you are incapacitated." Indeed, these documents are generally written so that these powers *are only granted while you are incapacitated* and unable to act on your own. These are called "springing" powers of attorney, because they spring into action upon your incapacity.

If you are elderly or facing a long-term illness, you may consider gently easing someone you trust into the role of your "agent," helping you through powers of attorney, over a period of time. This might be a sibling, a spouse, a child, or someone else you truly trust. This person should understand that if you have a stroke or other sudden decline, they will have to jump in with both feet.

If you think you may someday need to go further, and give full control to someone as conservator, you should *nominate* a person for that job too. This nomination is contained in the durable power of attorney for property (conservator of the estate nomination) and in the advance healthcare directive or durable power of attorney for healthcare (conservator of the person). These nominations may also be available in a separate document—apart from the durable powers of attorney for property or healthcare.

If it came to the need for a conservatorship—if, for example, you became a danger to yourself or others—a court would have to investigate and confirm your nomination. Your nominee would have to go through a criminal background check, a credit check, and more. But you would have had primary input. If you have not made a nomination, state laws indicate a priority of appointment typically based on your family tree and the laws of "intestate succession."

Regardless of the situation, clear your decision with your designees and nominees while you still can. It's a heavy responsibility to take on either power of attorney or to become a conservator, and you want to make sure everyone will agree to serve.

*Do not surprise a loved one with this responsibility after the stroke.* For one thing, they may say no. The Thirteenth Amendment to our United States Constitution thankfully abolished slavery. The precise language used is "involuntary servitude." You can never force someone to do something. They can always "just say no" and refuse to act.

If you are the person caring for someone with a mental incapacity, you may at some point have to consider a conservatorship. Sometimes, you simply have no other choice.

I know a woman who is taking care of her husband with dementia. He had always been a loving and gentle husband and father. But the disease is destroying his judgment, and little by little he is becoming violent. Recently, when they were in the drive-through line at a burger place, he just randomly let loose and clocked her. Knocked her out cold.

Now, it is truly her responsibility to go to court and apply for a conservatorship to have him institutionalized against his will. It happens.

In Mistake #9, we learned that living trusts are not generic, cut-and-paste documents. The same is true with power of attorney documents. For starters, you will be asked to grant separate powers for property and for healthcare decisions.

When you grant property power to your agent, you are authorizing this person to make decisions about your property and your finances while you are incapacitated—and to take specific responsibility for paying your bills, maintaining your online accounts, contributing to, managing, or withdrawing from your IRA, and the thousand other financial responsibilities we all face.

You may or may not, however, want this same person making healthcare decisions for you.

## DIVIDED POWERS FOR PROPERTY

You should also understand that even powers of attorney for property may be best divided.

If you own a business, you may want a different person to make business decisions during your incapacity than the person making your personal financial decisions.

You may want a different person making your investment decisions than the person handling your day-to-day finances.

You may also want to grant powers of attorney which are *not durable,* but end when you *lack* capacity. This may prevent, for example, a business partner from taking some action while you are out with a stroke.

*Nondurable* powers may empower a spouse or a business partner to make crucial decisions every time you are on vacation in remote locations, and then disempower them again when you return.

The term "non-durable" power of attorney or just plain "power of attorney" also means that the power that you give another is only valid while you are *not* incapacitated. For estate planning purposes, when you are planning for possible incapacity, you want to consider the "durable" kind of power of attorney because this particular power of attorney exists when you *are* incapacitated.

Another important question involves gifting. Most power of attorney documents I have seen do not include gifting authority—in other words, the agent you name during your incapacity generally does not have the right to give away your property to anyone else.

However, the power for one spouse to make a gift of their assets to another *may be crucial in public assistance benefit planning,* as you will see under "Monetary Fallbacks for Disability," below.

Work closely with your attorney to discuss these decisions and craft these documents. Consider your choices carefully—they may be the most important choices you ever make.

## DURABLE POWER OF ATTORNEY FOR HEALTHCARE (AKA ADVANCE HEALTHCARE DIRECTIVE)

If you are incapacitated with an illness, even if you are just under sedation for an hour-long operation—who do you trust to have your best interests at heart and make the right calls with doctors? Approve treatments? Argue with hospitals to keep you longer?

If you lose mental capacity due to stroke, dementia, Alzheimer's, Parkinson's, or other common conditions, who do you trust to move you from nursing facilities to home and back again?

Every one of us should choose a trusted person, *discuss the responsibilities with that person,* and update your choice as often as necessary. The power to make medical decisions for us when we cannot do so is called a "durable power of attorney for healthcare," and is granted through a pretty straightforward document.

The document says simply, "If I cannot make healthcare decisions for myself, then this person or these people can make them for me." You can name more than one person to serve jointly, or you can name them to serve consecutively. If this person cannot serve, then the power falls to the next, and etc.

Once again, a "power of attorney for healthcare" has nothing to do with the attorney writing the document. You can grant the healthcare power of attorney to anyone.

If you have a primary residence in one state and a vacation home in another, we recommend to our clients that they consider a durable power of attorney for healthcare for each state, because a lot of the related laws are state-specific.

## HIPAA AUTHORIZATION

A second document works closely with the power of attorney for healthcare decisions.

The Health Insurance Portability and Accountability Act

(HIPAA) created significant restrictions on who has access to your healthcare information. Although it boosted privacy, it also created barriers to swift decision-making and intervention by loved ones. If a doctor or hospital divulges your health information to someone without the proper authorization, they face huge fines—as much as $50,000 per violation, in some situations.

As a result, all health professionals and organizations take HIPAA rules very seriously.

The HIPAA authorization you sign gives authority to one or many people to have full access to your health information. As previously discussed in the Introduction, you may want to expand this authorization well beyond the person you have granted your power of attorney for healthcare. For example, you may want a home healthcare worker to be able to call up and check on your prescriptions, even if you don't want this person to make major medical decisions for you.

Think through your HIPAA authorizations carefully with an expert lawyer. In some cases, for example, you may want to have separate HIPAA authorization documents for different people and circumstances.

Although HIPAA is a federal law, there is no federal HIPAA form. Each state has its own. In my home state of California, for example, a HIPAA authorization must be printed in fourteen-point type to be valid!

## LIVING WILL VS. ADVANCE HEALTHCARE DIRECTIVE

A "living will," sometimes known as an "advance health-care directive," tells medical personnel, loved ones, and the person you have given power for healthcare decisions your preferences for medical care in dire circumstances, "in advance." A living will generally comes into play only when you are in the late stages of a fatal illness, fall into a coma, or have suffered an extremely serious injury.

Please do not confuse "living will" with "living trust." They are completely unrelated documents, with different purposes.

In most cases, the goal of a living will is to give permission to loved ones to let you pass away in order to avoid unnecessary suffering. Most living wills say, in essence, "If I'm a goner, let me go."

When my grandmother had a heart attack, my grandfather called the paramedics. It was a massive heart attack. The paramedics rushed over, got out their paddles, and shocked her heart back to "life." Then they put her on a ventilator and took her to the hospital. But she never recovered consciousness, and never showed signs of recovering the ability to breathe on her own. The doctors said there was no hope, and indeed, when I looked at her, I could see that her soul had probably already left her body.

My grandmother had created no living will and had never even discussed this possibility, so the decision to terminate life support was made even more difficult for my father and his two older brothers. After a week, my father and his brothers made the agonizing choice to terminate life support. Twenty years later, my father still asks me, "Did I do the right thing?"

I tell him that I was very close to my grandmother. And then I say, "Of course, you did." I say this because there really was no alternative. But the choice would have been much easier if she had made her own desires clear in a living will.

I will not go into all the specific details of a living will, or how it relates to "Do Not Resuscitate (DNR)" and "Physician Orders for Life-Sustaining Treatment (POLST)" orders. Instead, I refer you to your physician. Just make sure you get the appropriate legal and medical advice. Do, however, remember that a DNR/POLST is a *medical* order, where a living will is a *legal* document. Two very different items.

## PREFERENCES FOR FUNERALS AND DISPOSITION OF REMAINS
My wife has told me very clearly, "Now listen, when I die,

I don't want to be eaten by bugs. So, I want you to cremate me. I want you to put my ashes in a box and then into a columbarium where the family can come visit me."

I am glad she has told me this—and I take her words very seriously.

It's not easy to talk to your husband, much less your child about your possible illness and death. Usually, the children say, "Oh, Mom and Dad, you're going to live forever! We don't want to talk about that stuff." To them, it's almost as if talking about death might make it happen sooner.

But talk about death you must. Your estate plan should include instructions for your funeral and final disposition of remains. Instructions may include authorization for use of your body for organ donation, medical training, or research. You can also specify the nature of your funeral, and perhaps most importantly, who will make the decisions about your funeral.

Once again, failure to give instructions about funerals can lead to confusion and strife within a family.

Take the case of a woman I know who died with no plan, and five kids that hate each other. She had no durable power of attorney for healthcare, nor a living will with instructions for disposition of her remains. Her five children, of course, could not agree, so the funeral home *cremated the body and divided the ashes into five separate urns*—one for each of them to do with as they pleased. No kidding.

Remember, however, that writing a document is not a substitute for discussing the details with your loved ones in advance. When you become seriously ill or die, decisions will have to be made very rapidly, and the documents may not be available.

### DON'T FORGET THE POSSIBILITY OF PRE-NEED PLANNING

Your preparations may include pre-need planning, which I strongly recommend. With these arrangements, you go to a funeral home and pick everything out from the red carnations to the Studebaker-themed casket. Not to mention the white cake with strawberries and French crème filling to be served at the memorial service.

You can plan it all ahead and pay for it ahead of time. But you don't pay any monies directly to the funeral home— what if they are not around when the time comes? Instead, the money goes to an insurance company, which pays out a death benefit to cover these expenses at guaranteed rates.

Pre-need offers a pretty good deal, saves additional heartache, and makes the to-do list that much shorter when someone dies.

## THE ROLE OF THE LIVING TRUST IN INCAPACITY

As we saw in the case of Jack, a living trust may be even more important during your incapacity than it will be after you die.

Let's again begin by distinguishing between a will and a living trust. *A will is only valid at death. Before a death, a will is only a piece of paper.*

A living trust, on the other hand, is a *living* document which has binding legal effects from the moment it is signed. *It lives with you and helps you and your family throughout your lifetime.* Then, it continues to protect your estate and your loved ones after you die.

In Mistakes #9 and #10, we learned a lot about living trusts. If needed, go back and read those chapters now to see how a living trust creates a bucket for your assets, which can efficiently be passed into the control of others. You are the grantor of the trust, which exists for you as the beneficiary. While you are alive and capable, you are also the trustee, controlling the trust.

But in your living trust, you will designate a series of fallback trustees to take over when you die *or become incapacitated.* We lawyers call these people "successor trustees," or just "trustees" for short. The moment you are incapable of acting as trustee, another human being can immediately take over—whether it's your spouse, a child, a lawyer, a trust office of a bank, or whomever you choose. Using their powers as trustee, coordinated with the power of attorney for property you have granted to them or to others, this person can pay your bills, manage your investments, or whatever else needs to be done.

While you are alive, *your trustee can do this work only for your benefit*. Why? Because even though you are lying unconscious in a hospital, you are still the legal *beneficiary of the trust*. If the trustee uses the money for themselves then that's a theft crime and it's called embezzlement. People go to prison for embezzlement. It is one of the most serious property crimes in Anglo-American Law.

I should mention at this point that for a variety of legal and tax reasons, a living trust is not the appropriate bucket for certain kinds of assets, including annuities, IRAs, 401(k)s, 403(b)s, and TSA investments. Other vehicles are needed for those assets, and we will deal with them under Mistake #5. For now, however, you just need to know that a proper durable power of attorney for property can give the same person similar control over these other kinds of retirement plans and investments. That's why both kinds of documents must exist, and must be designed to work together.

Your attorney can also advise you on the use of an *irrevocable trust* as part of a strategy to obtain public assistance benefits such as Medicaid and certain Veterans Administration benefits to help pay for long-term care and nursing home bills.

### WHAT IF THE CAREGIVER DIES FIRST?

Few estate plans effectively deal with the common situation in which the caregiver, let's say the wife, dies before her sick husband. How common is this?

*Sixty percent of the time, the caregiving spouse dies before the sick spouse.* Got that? *Sixty percent of the time.*

At first, this statistic seems counterintuitive. Shouldn't the sick spouse die first? But think about it. Who is getting the proper nutrition? Who is going to their doctor appointments? Who is getting all the care? And who is getting worn out caring for the other?

Sadly, we often see this situation in our practice. Indeed, just to repeat the point, *we see it more often than not.* If you take away the cases in which the sick spouse has a terminal illness, the statistic is even higher.

Let me go back to the case of my grandmother. My grandfather was disabled for many years, and grandma took care of him with wonderful, diligent care. So diligent, that we had a running, albeit dark, joke in our family:

"Grandma, let's go have some fun this weekend."

"You go ahead," she'd say. "We'll have fun when your grandpa dies."

And we'd all laugh.

Well, she died in her eighties of that massive heart attack I discussed earlier. He lived to be ninety-three. I think that taking care of him literally wore her to death. I believe she did not take care of herself properly. It's hard for me to think about it any other way.

## MISTAKEN ASSUMPTIONS

Again and again, my firm sees situations in which one spouse, let's again say the husband, becomes incapacitated, and for a time, the married couple's lives together go on functioning with some normality. The wife can manage most things by herself. They have joint accounts, joint tenancy in property, and the wife muddles through to make healthcare decisions for her husband. The couple figures that when he dies, she'll still be in control of everything through their joint tenancy and joint accounts. So, they never get around to a formal estate plan.

*But what if the wife suddenly passes away?* Now, the husband lies helpless in his bed, without the mental capacity to manage his own affairs, and everything falls into chaos.

Like Jack in our example above, let's say this couple has a responsible daughter named Mary. This Mary is also willing to step in for her dad. But without a living trust naming her as trustee, and without a durable power of attorney, poor Mary will have to go to court and petition for a conservatorship. She will have to pay a lot of money to hire a lawyer. She will have to be investigated and approved.

Like Bob Jr. in Mistake #10, Mary will have to follow through in the same probate court, maybe in the same courtroom, but for a conservatorship. She will have to go to the courthouse and pass through the metal detectors. Thousands of dollars will have to be spent from the estate, not just to pay for the bills, the property taxes, even the funeral for Mom—but for court and attorney's fees. If the family assets are large, or some other interested party like a sibling tries to interfere, the amount may be tens or hundreds of thousands of dollars.

Meanwhile, Mary may grow frazzled and debilitated herself. She may have to give up a job to deal with this hassle. She may neglect her kids. She may endanger her relationship with her husband. In the Introduction, I said, "It's Not about the Money (But It Is about the Money)." In cases like this, it may start out about the money, but in the end, it will be about the hassle. People would often happily give up their inheritance to be rid of the burdens which a death or disability has dropped in their lap.

## MONETARY FALLBACKS FOR DISABILITY

When you talk to estate planning attorneys, they will tell you plenty of stories in which a frazzled man or woman has come into their office and said, "I'm done. I can't handle it anymore. I've been taking care of my spouse for four years, and I'm physically worn out. I'm emotionally drained. What can I do?"

Like my grandma, these folks have been the primary caregivers for people who cannot bathe themselves. Cannot use the toilet. Cannot feed themselves. People who may stay up all night and sleep all day. Who have numerous doctors' appointments which require difficult trips in wheelchairs and special transportation. On top of that, it's very hard to see someone you have created a life with slowly fade away.

Even a strong, young person would find it difficult to provide this care. But often, these heroic caregivers are in their seventies, eighties, or even nineties. They come in to an estate planning office to find out how they can institutionalize their spouse. "I have to do this today," they say. "It's over. Help me figure this out."

Most people cannot afford $3,000 to $30,000 or more a

month for board and care or skilled nursing facilities. When they try, they often end up impoverishing themselves in the process. Just because one spouse moves into an institution, it doesn't mean that the basic expenses of the other spouse are greatly reduced. And what if both spouses become disabled?

Many people assume that the government will step in to help with long-term care. But most government programs provide help *only when you become truly impoverished*— generally defined as having less than $2,000 to just under $15,000 for single people, and just over $100,000 for couples, in total assets depending on which state you live in. Programs may also be available for veterans and surviving spouses of wartime veterans. This is called "aid and attendance."

### HOW ESTATE PLANNING CAN HELP

It's beyond the scope of this book to explore all the options for long-term care. Every situation is different, and you need to do a lot of research. But proper estate planning using a qualified attorney who understands such issues can open up important options.

For example, using a durable power of attorney for property, we can sometimes move assets completely out of a sick spouse's name into the spouse's name who is not sick, so that the sick spouse can qualify for public assistance benefits and move into a nursing facility. Meanwhile, the well spouse can stay at home, often with much or all income and assets intact. As noted above, however, these powers of attorney must include gifting rights, which are not commonly included in such documents.

The government generally does not object to these transfers of assets or punish you for making them, because they really do not want the surviving spouse to be impoverished by paying for long-term care. Once impoverished, he or she becomes an additional burden on the public good.

But there are very low limitations on what can be transferred without triggering a period of disqualification for public assistance benefits. If either spouse has more assets, then the transfers may result in a period of ineligibility.

Again, an irrevocable trust will often be used as part of this planning strategy.

If such instruments are already in place before the disabled spouse loses mental competence, such an action may be fairly simple. Wait too long, and you will have to go through a court proceeding to get these powers, with less predictable results. In fact, many judges will not grant orders transferring assets of someone who has lost mental capacity.

Please do not make the common mistake of assuming spouses have the power to make these significant legal moves just because they have joint bank accounts or joint tenancy in a house. To actually move titles to real property, change the form of assets, and alter the character of ownership, requires advanced legal planning and specific documents—or a court order.

For example, if a wife wanted to take full ownership of a rental house to protect it from being counted as an asset for her husband, she might have to go to court and apply for the appropriate court order transferring the rental house to her. If her husband had simply signed a durable power of attorney *with gifting authority* for her in advance, no such court action would likely be necessary.

Of course, different states may offer greatly differing legal opportunities, definitions of indigence, and public benefits. And you absolutely need an expert attorney with specific training in such issues. To move assets around to protect spouses, *you cannot use a "general purpose lawyer."* Even most estate planning attorneys have little to no competence in this realm, sometimes called "elder law." It's a specialty within a specialty.

For more advice on choosing an attorney, please see the Introduction.

## WHAT ABOUT LONG-TERM CARE INSURANCE?

You will find two schools of thought about long-term care insurance. One school says that everyone should buy a policy. The other says that your premium money would be better invested elsewhere.

You should certainly investigate any long-term insurance policy closely, as it must be considered in relation to your particular circumstances. I recommend clients discuss the subject with their financial advisor and other appropriate stakeholders before taking any action.

Long-term care insurance will cover you if you can't take care of yourself in very specific ways. Unfortunately, most policies do not cover 100 percent of the costs, and they generally have significant limitations. For example, policies often require a waiting period in which you have to be sick for perhaps ninety days before they kick in. Complications on this provision often arise related to dates of discharge from one facility to another, from rehab to board and care, or from Medicare to private insurance, etc. These technicalities often delay the start of your long-term care benefit—making it impossible to access your policy when you need it most.

In addition, these policies often include a lifetime cap, meaning they may only cover "long-term care" for three or four years.

Usually, they also include daily maximums which may not allow for the kind of care or facility you require. Even worse, your daily maximum may not be tied to an inflation index which increases over time. The maximum may be a flat rate, meaning that if you bought a policy twenty years ago that paid a flat $100 a day, it won't cover a contemporary facility charging $300 a day plus extras (and there are always extras). You will have to make up the difference.

Bottom line: *just because you buy a long-term care policy does not mean you are covered for long-term care.* Do plenty of homework and get professional advice before you sign on the dotted line.

# #7

# FAILING TO PROTECT BENEFICIARIES FROM THEMSELVES

———

Do you care if your beneficiaries screw up their lives after you are gone? What if your legacy *enables* them to screw up their lives? Earlier I explained that in the absence of other arrangements in a properly constructed trust, a child will fully inherit their portion of your estate at age eighteen. I mentioned how that might not be such a great idea (see Mistake #10).

Let me repeat my opinion: very few eighteen-year-olds know how to handle money, including that $100,000 college fund you left in your will.

Do you remember the fund you described with beautiful words about "helping light their bright future?"

You and I are aware that $100,000 in today's dollars will provide a great boon to any student, but may not be enough to cover even two years at a private university. To a kid, however, it may seem like the proverbial pot of gold at the end of the rainbow. It may seem like $100 million. A kid with that kind of money may think they can go out and party, or run up credit card bills like an NFL star (another group not famous for financial management).

I remember how one day I got a call from a car dealership about an almost-eighteen-year-old I'll call Johnny. The manager of the place got on the line. He said, "I've got a kid named Johnny standing here, and he tells me he's going to inherit a hundred grand in two days. You're his attorney, right?"

I take a deep breath and confirm that I am, indeed, his attorney.

"Well, can you confirm that he's going to get all that money in two days? If so, we'll let him drive this new convertible off the lot right now."

"Put Johnny on the phone," I replied.

"Hey, Mr. Cunningham!" said Johnny, all bright and eager.

"Johnny," I said. "What the hell are you doing? You haven't even inherited the money yet and you're already blowing it? Do you understand that you have to *live* on that money? That you have to *go to school* on that money? You are not rich, Johnny. It is not that much money. Get your butt out of there."

I know that folks can have two points of view about their legacy. The first says, "I can't worry so much about my children once I'm dead. They'll be adults. I'll be gone. I won't care." The second says, "I've worked too long and too hard for what I've accumulated. I don't want it blown."

In my experience, about half the people who inherit blow their inheritance pretty much right away. Poof, it's gone.

In the case of Johnny, he'd technically inherited the money when he was only ten years old, but it had been sitting in a bank account collecting interest. During those eight years, the bequest no doubt provided a delightful obsession for his teenage imagination. A ten-year-old cannot, by law, control his or her own money. If no financial guardian has been nominated by a will or living trust, the court will provide one at great expense to the estate. But when the child reaches eighteen, they get access to whatever is left.

I should mention that for a small amount of money, such as $100,000, a simple "blocked account" can be an inexpensive alternative to a trust with an assigned guardian. In that case, a bank simply holds the money until the child turns eighteen.

In either case, unless you have made other arrangements, there's nothing that anyone—including a judge—can do to stop a kid from walking into the bank on his or her eighteenth birthday with a photo ID, taking out the money, and buying a Porsche.

And believe me, it happens every day.

## TRUST YOUR TRUST, NOT THE PERSON

In my opinion, you should not trust your young or irresponsible beneficiary. You should trust your trust.

When you sit down to discuss a living trust with your estate planning attorney, you need to talk through the personalities and outcomes for each of your beneficiaries. I provide examples of such conversations in Mistake #6.

We have talked about living trusts as "buckets" into which you put your assets, in order to pass them on in an orderly way. If you have dependents who cannot handle their own affairs, you need to think about creating a bucket with a little spigot attached.

The spigot will be controlled by the responsible adult you name as trustee until your beneficiary turns twenty-two, twenty-five, thirty, fifty, or *never*, depending on what you know about that beneficiary.

Such a bucket, properly constructed by a reliable attorney, cannot be dumped out on the ground and wasted all at once. Instead, the spigot pays out $500 a month, $1,000 a month, or whatever makes sense to you. Importantly, those amounts may be easier for your financially inexperienced heirs to visualize, hence, manage. A hundred thousand dollars can be a mere abstraction, hard to comprehend. Everyone understands a thousand a month.

Of course, it's crucial that you assign a trustee who can handle the responsibility of controlling your little spigot. You must also anticipate such issues as a trustee who can no longer serve. We look more deeply into these issues in Mistake #3: Assuming Your Trustee Will Know What to Do.

Earlier I talked about the remarkable freedom that Americans have to control what happens to their stuff after they die. One of these freedoms allows us to protect our irresponsible heirs from themselves. Each trust can be highly tailored to individual circumstances.

It's your money, and you get to decide.

For example, you can say that an heir will get no access to their funds until they hit, say, forty. Along the way, prior to age forty, the money can be dripped out to them on an as-needed basis, in a controlled manner by the assigned trustee. I've seen trusts structured so that a child receives a third at age twenty-five, a third at age thirty, and a third at age thirty-five (which for technical reasons must be written as "a third, a half, and a whole").

What does such an arrangement accomplish? Well, for the under-motivated child, it might force them to work, while giving them really useful boosts at key moments in their careers. Like our friend with the troubled child in Mistake #9, you may be asking yourself, "If my son gets the money right away, will he just sit around smoking dope and playing video games all day?"

I have plenty of clients who tell me their kids have reached fifty, but they still can't be trusted to handle large amounts of cash. And to be frank: if someone has reached fifty without achieving financial responsibility, it's unlikely they ever will.

## HEIRS MIGHT BETTER APPRECIATE A STIPEND

In the above examples, you may worry that there's something mean-spirited in structuring a trust to provide a stipend instead of a lump sum. But in my experience, such a legacy often creates a far more positive memory—even for an older heir.

It's all in how you phrase it.

Suppose you and your husband are eighty-five. You sit down with your daughter who is fifty-nine. She has worked hard her whole life, but she's never been that great with money, and hasn't put much away. She's tired out and doesn't want to work forever, but she's worried about her retirement. Suppose you tell her, "Listen, honey, we're setting up a trust. After we're gone, this trust will pay you $1,000 a month, hopefully for the rest of your life."

Think what joy that would give her. "Wow, $1,000 a month for the rest of my life? That's awesome! Thanks, Mom and Dad!"

Then every single month, when that payment rolls in from your living trust to her bank account, your daughter thinks of Mom and Dad with fondness. You are remembered every month. And you can rest easier, knowing that no matter what happens, she will have something to live on.

On the other hand, if you just gave her $200,000 in a lump sum, it's a one-time event. She may make a foolish investment, or worse. Ten years later, both you and the lump sum will be just a memory.

Such arrangements can be set up with a properly drafted, continuing trust that names a responsible successor trustee—a person, private professional fiduciary, or bank. Or, you could simply buy an annuity that pays her a guaranteed monthly dividend. Discuss these options with your attorney and financial planner.

The same positive attitude should be taken with other heirs for whom you create a bucket with a "spigot." You can create a tremendous investment advantage by keeping money in a trust fund which is properly managed to grow over time. So, if you think it's wise to withhold monies from an heir until twenty-five, thirty, thirty-five or beyond, you can and should frame this arrangement in a positive light. "In order to provide Johnny with more substantial means, we have created a trust, named Premier Trust Company in Nevada, invested with Ascent Wealth Management to grow over the next twenty years. Increasing payments will be made to Johnny when he turns twenty-five, thirty, and thirty-five." You need say nothing about any lack of confidence in Johnny's judgment.

Think about a trust with delayed distribution as a caterpillar that becomes a butterfly over time. Focus on the butterfly.

## PROTECTING HEIRS WITH DISABILITIES

More and more Americans find themselves with long-term

responsibility for adults with disabilities or diminished capacity. These might be dependents who had special needs from birth, or they might be elderly relatives suffering from Alzheimer's or other mentally disabling conditions.

Indeed, these days, many estate plans consider the deceased's parents as well as their children.

You must, of course, create plans which will ensure that the right people maintain control of both the property and the "persons" of disabled dependents. This is true whether the person is mentally capable of handling their own finances or merely suffers from a serious physical disability.

In all cases, the financial issues related to caring for disabled dependents are complex, and must be handled by an experienced attorney. (See Mistake #8 for more about planning for your own disability.)

For example, even a very modest inheritance may threaten the continuation of certain needs-based public assistance benefits, with potentially catastrophic results. Your attorney must know, for example, that SSDI (Social Security Disability Income) allows for the inheritance of monies without any problem. But SSI (Supplemental Security Income) does not, because it is a needs-based benefit.

In short, you and your attorney must not simply give

someone with a disability $100,000 without doing some serious homework. First, they may not be able to handle that money properly. But second, you may actually be doing them harm.

A good estate attorney can structure a "special needs trust" or a "supplemental needs trust" to help a disabled beneficiary, *depending on the state in which the beneficiary resides—not the state in which you reside*. The state is crucial, as laws vary. When properly constructed, such a trust will not be "owned" by the beneficiary, and hence will not threaten their benefits, but can still pay them a supplemental income, administered by a trustee.

In such situations, the supplemental income can usually be used only for needs other than food, clothing, and shelter. If it *is* used for food, clothing or shelter, it can reduce the monthly benefit check amount.

## THE ROLE OF THE TRUST PROTECTOR

Any time you are providing for a beneficiary with disabilities, I think it's vital to include a "trust protector" in your estate plan. This role can be played by anyone, though most often, it's played by a legal professional or law firm. You should know that a court *always* has powers over the trust and trustee. With a trust protector, those powers are in part moved from the court to an individual.

This means a trust protector is a person who has limited control over the trust, but is not the trustee.

The idea of the trust protector came from the English. It became a popular part of American law during the 1990s, because it solved a vital problem in estate planning: *what if your trust must be changed after your death?*

In many cases, it would be completely inappropriate for either the beneficiary or the trustee to be given power guardianship to make such changes. The beneficiary may not be competent, and the trustee may not be fully trusted to do such radical surgery, which may include modifying the way a trust is paid out or administered. Indeed, most trusts must be written so they are *irrevocable* and *unamendable* following the grantor's (creator's) death.

But guess what? In current law, a trust protector *can* be named within the trust document who can modify some of the terms, even of an irrevocable trust. Trust protectors have become a common feature of many trusts created by up-to-date attorneys.

What may trigger the intervention of a trust protector? First, someone involved must step forward and request that the trust protector take action. The trust protector is not omniscient and will not be checking in from time to time. But someone, such as a guardian, may see, for example, that a beneficiary who is disabled or has special needs will be moving to another state with very different laws and public benefits systems. This guardian may ask the trust protector to amend the trust to take into account the new system. In another case, a trustee will realize that he or she can no longer serve, and appeal to the trust protector to name a new trustee. Or, important tax changes must be made to account for new tax laws.

If a trust protector has been named in the trust, it is as simple for the trust protector to make these limited technical changes as it is for a mechanic to adjust a piece of machinery by turning a screw. Without a trust protector in place, everyone has to go to court. The power of the trust protector does not extend to major changes, such as changing the beneficiary to an inheritance.

One major function of a trust protector is to remove a bad trustee. A beneficiary may complain to the trust protector that a trustee has become dangerously irresponsible and then appeal to the protector for a change of trustee. Without a trust protector in place, such a change may easily require a year to complete through the courts.

### PLANNING FOR CHANGE

Trust and probate law goes through major shifts pretty much every year. Sometimes every day. In fact, each new probate case published in the Court of Appeals or Supreme Court could potentially affect probate law.

As discussed elsewhere, an "irrevocable trust" will be absolutely necessary to create certain legal mechanisms (see for example the case of Kevin, in Mistake #6). But, if a trust has been written in stone as irrevocable and unamendable, it's very expensive and time consuming to change it if you don't have a trust protector. The trustee or beneficiary will have to go through a lengthy court proceeding, which is exactly what you wanted to avoid by creating an estate plan in the first place.

It's very common in our practice to see adult disabled children relocate to another state when their parents die. Relatives often live across the country, or the right kind of facility may be available only across state lines. In such cases, we have to look at modifying a special needs or supplemental needs trust. Courts are a hassle. When you use a Trust Protector it takes the place of a court and saves time, minimizes hassles, and saves money. We're talking about a couple hundred dollars instead of $10,000 or more to modify the terms of the trust. Without a trust protector, the trustee may have to go to court to modify the trust, which is a big hassle and costs money and time. With a trust protector, the result is no court, no wasted money, and no wasted time.

Make sure to discuss the possible need for a trust protector with your attorney. We'll learn about the trust protector's role in Mistake #6: Letting Third Parties Take Advantage of Your Beneficiaries.

## LOOKING AHEAD TO CONSEQUENCES

In this chapter, we've seen how a living trust can function twenty, thirty, fifty years or more after your death. Indeed, your living trust truly has a life of its own, and may survive well beyond the second or third generation.

Some states have laws which say, in essence, "A trust can't go on forever." In other states, a trust can literally continue in perpetuity—in fact, it can continue so long that the language in the trust may become obsolete. Grammar may have significantly evolved since it was first written.

But, we've also seen how trusts, *no matter how well intentioned,* can have both negative and positive impacts for your heirs as their mechanisms play out through the years. In the next chapter, we'll look at more ways to protect your legacy—and how you can make sure your estate plan always does more good than harm.

MISTAKE

# LETTING THIRD PARTIES TAKE ADVANTAGE OF YOUR BENEFICIARIES

In the last chapter, we talked about protecting your heirs, also known in legalese as "beneficiaries," from themselves. But maybe you don't have to worry about such protections. Maybe none of your heirs are young and foolish. Perhaps none are mentally incapacitated. All might be gainfully employed and out of prison. Maybe you can rely on them to handle even a large bequest. You may even have the *perfect* family.

Unfortunately, however, it's a rough world out there, and

lots of third parties can prey on even the most responsible heir. You should protect your legacy as best you can from such persons.

Who are these third parties? In this chapter, we'll discuss both creditors and professional estate predators. But let's start with the most common of dangerous third parties: divorced spouses.

## DIVORCE

No matter how much we all wish it were not true, about 50 percent of marriages end in divorce. And in 100 percent of divorce cases, the structure of marital property matters. So does the structure of any inheritance either spouse may receive.

How are the marriages of your beneficiaries?

Suppose, when you die, your estate generously gifts $500,000 to your wonderful niece, Sandra. After your funeral, when your will is read, Sandra loves you all the more. During payout by the executor, the money passes quickly into Sandra's joint bank account with her husband.

So far, so good.

But what if, a short month later, Sandra's husband files for divorce? Has that $500,000 suddenly become marital property and fair game in the divorce proceeding? Maybe, and maybe not. What if Sandra and her husband put that money directly into paying off the mortgage on their house—but the house goes to the husband in the eventual divorce settlement? Has Sandra lost most or all benefit from the $500,000 you left her? Very possibly, yes.

Even worse, the receipt of that $500,000 *may trigger the divorce itself.* Why? Because suddenly, a frustrated spouse sees a financial path out of the marriage. He or she makes the move.

Honestly, it happens all the time.

I recently had a case in which a client was owed a sum of exactly $500,000 from a bequest. Even though he had set up a separate account in his own name, the money was mistakenly wired to his joint bank account. That same week, his wife filed for divorce and succeeded in taking half the money.

Indeed, it's a sad fact that statistically, *when there's more money floating around, people are more likely to get divorced.* When the economy went down in 2008, we saw a period with fewer divorces, simply because people could not afford to get divorced. When the economy went back up, so did the divorce rate.

In another case, I was called as a witness on a case involving a client who was inheriting a big chunk of money. The judge wanted to know how much he was inheriting, and he wanted to delve into the precise nature of the estate documents, because the court might want to impose a higher order of spousal support on my client. In this case, the living trust documents proved bulletproof, and the inheritance could not be counted in my client's assets.

Nevertheless, the ex-wife gave it her best shot.

Laws vary by state, but in general, if (and only if) an inheritance has been properly structured through a trust, it does not become part of marital property, and it can be protected from loss during a divorce.

## CREDITORS AND PREDATORS

You must also create a trust in a manner that will protect your heirs from unworthy creditors and professional predators.

I'm not talking about people or businesses to whom your heirs have stopped paying bills. I firmly believe in paying money that is owed. I'm talking about the many ways in which your heirs may become responsible for something *not their fault at all.*

Thanks to the way we've set up our society and our legal system, this also happens all the time. America comprises about 5 percent of the world's population, yet we file 95 percent of the world's lawsuits.

Maybe your heir cosigns for a student loan for his child—and when the kid turns forty, your long-suffering heir is still responsible for the money. Maybe another heir becomes a business partner in a venture that goes under, thanks to crazy debts created by her partner.

Maybe, as in the example in Mistake #9, your heir runs an apartment building in which a bad manager sparks a lawsuit by a protected class of tenant.

Maybe your heir is a surgeon and a patient's lawyer finds a way to go beyond her malpractice insurance to attack her personal assets.

Many times, people are held liable for things which are not what any normal person would consider their responsibility. But creditors, predators, and courts do. Indeed, people are often pulled into lawsuits which honestly baffle them.

A physician works as part of a team in an operating room, and hours after she's done her part of the job and left the hospital, something completely unrelated goes wrong. Usually, the patient's attorney will sue her along with everyone else, including the anesthesiologist, the hospital, everyone—figuring someone will be nailed for the money. The same may be true if you are a part owner of a business that you do not manage personally.

As lawyers, we are taught to split "causation" between the people who actually cause the harm and the people who don't necessarily cause the harm but can still be held legally responsible for the harm. One employee punches another employee? The employer may be held liable.

In my noble profession, legal strategies often revolve not around who did the deed, but who has money to pay for the consequences. Unless you do your estate planning right, you can make your heirs into targets, just by giving them your hard-earned stash.

## WHO ARE THE PREDATORS?

Beyond creditors and lawyers, we see professional predators who actively seek out money from estates, especially if those estates go to probate. Remember that once in probate, the names of all estate beneficiaries and all the details of the finances are made public—right down to the date each person inherits and the specific amount of that inheritance, (see Mistake #10: Letting Your Family Go to Probate).

Professional predators gather probate information, and then show up with scams of all kinds, from land deals to bogus lawsuits. They might appear right at the probate hearing, with some surprise debt you yourself might not have remembered if you had been alive and standing there in front of the judge.

Then there's the government. Governmental agencies and their lawyers are just like everyone else: they look for significant piles of money and go after them. Their tactics may include everything from estate "death" taxes to collecting income taxes on inherited IRA distributions (see Mistake #5: Assuming Your Living Trust Covers Things Like IRAs, 401(k)s, 403(b)s, 457s, Annuities, and Insurance). I'm a patriotic guy, but as a lawyer protecting my clients, I have to list the IRS under "predators," too.

## BANKRUPTCY

Bankruptcy can lead to equally problematic inheritances.

Here's an all too common situation. A man dies and our office contacts his beneficiary to say, "We are ready to give you your $200,000 from the estate."

There's a pause at the other end of the line, and the unhappy heir says, "Okay, but can you not give me that money for about six months?"

"Why is that?"

"Well, I'm in the middle of bankruptcy. Once my bankruptcy trustee finds out about this money, he's going to take it and pay my creditors. I won't see a penny. If you wait, I can use that money to start over."

The situation can be worse if the asset is something not easily subdivided, like a house or a business. In such cases, the bankruptcy trustee can come in, step into the shoes of the inheriting child, and become a stakeholder in the process, with a lot of say. The house may go into a forced sale. A lien may be attached to the profits of the business.

Because bankruptcy court is federal, it can override what the state court wants to do or decides should be done. Federal bankruptcy court can effectively overrule the probate court, the trust court, or the trustee.

## THE HIGH-MAINTENANCE SPOUSE

As an attorney, I sometimes have to push honesty into the "brutal" category. Here is one of those cases. Under the predators who can destroy an estate, I am going to list "high-maintenance spouses."

What's a high-maintenance spouse? It's a husband or wife who really, *really* likes to spend money, especially your heir's inherited money. Such a spouse can be found on any rung of the socio-economic ladder—rich, poor, middle-class, it doesn't seem to matter.

We're not talking about divorce here, we're talking about the unintended consequences of marriage.

One time, a woman found me after I spoke at a seminar, and said, "Jim, I have a Jane."

I knew what she meant. In the seminar, I had used the example of "Jane" as an heir with a husband who really liked to spend money.

"Ah," I said. "Tell me about Jane."

"Well, when my daughter inherited about $300,000 from her dad, and her husband got hold of it. He bought a truck, a bass boat, and partied until the money was gone." She paused. "Seriously, *all* that money's gone."

"I'm so sorry," I said. Coming from a rural town, I know a guy can easily blow $300,000 on a truck and a bass boat.

"Now, my daughter has come to me and said, 'Mom, I don't want the same thing to happen again when you die and leave me money. I'm sixty years old. I've been working hard my whole life waiting tables and doing housecleaning. I'm worn out. I can't work anymore. Mom, will you please set up your estate plan in a way that protects me?'"

I was blown away by this conversation. It's pretty rare that a beneficiary has that kind of self-awareness, along with the humble wisdom to come to her mom for advance planning in this way.

I set up a trust in this woman's estate plan that held about a million dollars for Jane's benefit. *But Jane herself could not remove any of the money,* because someone else was the trustee for her funds. We figured that if the million were properly invested, Jane could take out 4.8 percent, or $48,000 a year. The language of the trust permitted Jane to receive $4,000 a month—plenty for Jane to live on, within her lifestyle.

And since she herself was blocked from accessing the money, her husband could never pressure her for another big purchase.

Jane's reaction was superb. "Oh, my goodness. That's such a blessing," she said. "I've never even made $4,000 in a month while working. Now I know I'm going to be comfortable. Now I know I'm safe and secure. If my husband gets hold of that $4,000 this month, I'll know I've got *another* $4,000 coming in next month. It's not like he's going to go through the whole million dollars. Ever. This makes me feel so happy and safe as a daughter."

The client was equally thrilled. She said, "Wow, now I know I'm providing for my daughter. She's in a tough situation that she can't get out of, but at least I've made it easier instead of harder."

Other lawyers call a trust like this a "general needs trust." I like to think of it as a "dole-it-out trust." You dole a little bit of money out every month to Jane for the rest of her life. Result: she is protected from a predator.

## ALAN AND KEVIN GET IT RIGHT

Now let's talk about an heir who has already had a lot of financial success in his life. Maybe he's a physician with a substantial net worth, along with a house, investments, and other assets. He may also have, perhaps, a "high-maintenance" spouse, or even an unstable spouse. Let's call him Kevin. And his wife, we'll call Melanie.

Kevin's father, Alan, was even more successful than his son. He's planning on leaving Kevin a tidy sum in the millions, but he knows that Kevin always faces significant threats to his wealth. For starters, as a physician, Kevin always faces the possibility of huge lawsuits. He also dabbles in side businesses with partners who may go after him for business debts.

Then there's the unpredictable Melanie. Last year, without any notice, she took a trip to Paris with an old friend and spent a fortune at shops on La Rive Droite. First-class flights, the works. By the end of her trip, clerks at the Hermès mothership on Rue du Faubourg Saint-Honoré were greeting Melanie by name. She and Kevin had another of their many huge arguments afterwards, and both father and son know that if the couple keeps fighting, a divorce is not hard to imagine.

Alan and Kevin go to a good attorney, and he sets up a remarkable trust for just their situation. It's an innovative vehicle I call an "inheritance protection trust," or IPT.

In this case, instead of Kevin inheriting his father's money outright, it goes into the separate bucket of a trust. Like some of the other buckets we discussed, including the "dole-it-out" trust above, this bucket has a spigot to control distributions. The bucket also has a tight lid.

During Alan's lifetime, this trust operates like any living trust. Alan, as both trustee and beneficiary, has full control to use it as he pleases. But when Alan dies, Alan's trust goes through a metamorphosis:

It becomes a different, irrevocable, separate bucket. A bucket with a tight lid.

Like Jane's dole-it-out trust, this strong IPT bucket includes a spigot to let money out in a controlled way. Unlike Jane's trust, however, Kevin is the initial trustee and always remains the beneficiary. He both benefits from the trust *and while things are okay,* controls the trust. Because the trust is irrevocable, it creates the foundation of an asset protection for Kevin—something Kevin cannot do so easily on his own. Alan must, however, set it up in advance for Kevin. The trust cannot be changed, and Kevin cannot add his own assets to Alan's IPT.

If the trust were revocable, it could never offer asset protection, because the law would deem those assets to be the property of Kevin.

The only person who can reach into the IPT bucket and get any money out is the trustee. Currently, Kevin is the trustee. If he wants some money to go to Paris with Melanie, it's there for him. He can stroll into Hermès with her and be greeted by name and finally buy her that crocodile Birkin bag she's been coveting. But only he is entitled to the money, not her.

If Kevin gets drawn into a malpractice suit, lawyers can try, but they won't get this trust money. Why? Because Kevin does not own the money, the trust does. As the trust is *irrevocable*—it cannot be changed to give the plaintiff access.

And chances are, when the dust settles, Kevin will be able to settle with the disappointed party for pennies on the dollar.

If he gets attacked by undeserving creditors through his business investments, the creditors cannot get hold of this money, either. Indeed, Kevin could even declare bankruptcy without including this trust money in his assets—because the money is not his.

And yes, if Kevin and Melanie get a divorce, that money's not in Kevin's name, only in the name of the trust. It's not marital property, because only married *people* can have marital property.

Kevin's trust money has been protected from all predators, but Kevin could still spend all of that money during his lifetime if he wanted. When he dies, this trust can be written so that what's left goes to his kids, tax-free—even though he has piles of other money to pass on.

Important to this particular kind of trust, *the original money was not Kevin's, but Alan's.* This follows an important principal in law which says that basically, *whatever you can get, your creditors can get.* Generally, you cannot set up a trust like this on your own using your own money, and suddenly achieve asset protection for yourself. But through the right estate plan, it is indeed possible to give this protection to your heirs.

To make this trust function properly will also require a trust protector. We learned a little about trust protectors earlier, in Mistake #7. And we'll learn more in the chapters to come. But in essence, a trust protector is a substitute for a judge and a court. As noted earlier, a trust protector has power over the trust, but is not a trustee. They have the power to make *limited* changes to a trust, including removing or adding trustees. They cannot change the current or future beneficiaries, but they can make their limited changes even to an "irrevocable trust."

In some circumstances, to protect himself from creditors, Kevin may need to pick up the phone and call the trust protector. He'll say, "Hey, Mr. Trust Protector, will you please remove me as trustee and appoint my best friend, Tom, as trustee?"

The trust protector will have the power to make that change. Then Tom can exercise his discretion as the new trustee and not distribute Kevin any money. Interestingly, even though Tom is now holding on to the bucket, Kevin still has the right *as an individual* to get money from the bucket. This may seem contradictory, but that's how the law's written: Kevin's inheritance is protected. But once Kevin pulls any money out, of course, that money will no longer be protected—so he should spend it fast.

Creating an inheritance protection trust can be an entirely legitimate strategy under the law. But obviously, you need an expert attorney in estate planning to do it right.

## DON'T LEAVE THEM ANYTHING?

A fellow lawyer once said, "If you love someone, don't leave them anything." After reading the examples in this chapter, you may now understand his joke.

He was not referring to the angst associated with money. He was referring to the fact that *whatever is actually in your name, someone else can take from you.* A divorce court can take it. A predator. A creditor. A free-spending spouse. If you need to protect your heirs, you should consider putting your legacy into the separate bucket of a trust.

A properly constructed trust can offer your heirs a lot of protection after you are gone. It can build a moat and a wall around the assets. In the case of Jane, she did not "own" the million dollars. It was owned by a dole-it-out trust for her benefit, controlled by a friendly third-party—not her husband. In the case of Kevin, he had much more control, but was still merely the beneficiary, not the owner of his father's legacy.

But to pull this kind of thing off, you *must* get your living trust right—the first time. Don't assume that anything is "generic," and for heaven's sake, use an attorney. Still need convincing? (See Mistake #9: Assuming All Living Trust Plans Are the Same.)

*MISTAKE*

# #5

# ASSUMING YOUR LIVING TRUST COVERS THINGS LIKE IRAS, 401(K)S, 403(B)S, 457S, ANNUITIES, AND INSURANCE

---

Earlier in the book, I talked about the importance of knowing what you don't know—and believe me, you don't know nearly enough about your Individual Retirement Account, or IRA.

IRAs offer enormous, but usually untapped financial opportunities. Byzantine deadlines. Land mines for heirs. Huge differences in strategy depending on your age, the age of your heirs, and the exact birthdays of everyone involved. Different rules apply for the disabled, the chronically ill, spouses, people who inherit your IRA who are less than 10 years younger than you, and minor children under age 18 (or in school up to the age of 26).

In short, IRAs are more complicated than you could possibly imagine in your wildest dreams. I'm not overstating the case when I call *IRAs in America* a fiscal drama of Shakespearean proportions with a dash of Orwell. Plot points include brutal IRS penalties, common errors by ignorant estate attorneys, and catastrophic decisions made by 87 percent of heirs.

*Spoiler alert:* just because it's an IRA, it doesn't mean you can ignore taxes. Unless it's a Roth IRA, *all* the money that comes out of the IRA is subject to income taxes. But both Roth IRAs and "non-Roth" IRAs are subject to death taxes.

Just because you socked away all that money, don't assume you or your heirs will get to keep it.

## THE JOURNEY FROM ERISA TO IRA

If you think you can avoid this drama because you don't have an IRA, but you have a 401(k), you are wrong. When I use the term IRA in the discussion below, I mean to include *all* tax-advantaged retirement accounts, including those created under ERISA, the Employee Retirement Income Security Act. These include IRAs but also include 401(k)s, 403(b)s, TSAs, TSPs, 457s, etc.—a whole litany of possibilities. These accounts are collectively called "qualified" accounts because they are tax-advantaged accounts that qualify for deferment of taxes under law.

It's a good idea to consider rolling each kind of ERISA or tax-advantaged account into an IRA upon separation from an employer. The biggest reason is that although federal law permits people who inherit a 401(k), for example, to do some pretty awesome tax-deferral planning, many of the employers' plans themselves do not permit such planning. For example, these plans often do not permit your heirs to stretch out distributions over ten years, or even a lifetime, like an IRA. Instead, most require heirs to take out the money over a five-year period following the death of the owner of the 401(k).

People may also put away money into something like a "cash balance pension plan," which can allow some to sock away over $200,000 a year pretax—but eventually, that money should also be rolled over to an IRA to create the actual pension.

That's why, for the sake of simplicity, I will focus on IRAs in my discussion of tax-advantaged retirement accounts.

Most retirement account paths eventually lead to IRA rules, though the timing of each move must be carefully planned with an expert.

## USING THE MAGIC OF TAX DEFERRAL

The basic idea of IRAs, or any tax-advantaged accounts, is straightforward enough. All these vehicles were invented so that people could create their own retirement plans by deferring taxes on some of their earned income until a future date when their incomes would be lower.

In other words, IRAs are about patience: already a problem for most people.

In many ERISA plans, you make pretax contributions of money to savings and investment accounts that you will later access when you retire: at which time, you will have to pay taxes at your then-current, presumably lower rates.

If you have a regular job, you can often put away a chunk of your salary up to a certain dollar amount every year. Sometimes, your company chips in something too. If you're self-employed, you can make your own contributions.

Advice on how to invest your IRA varies from plan to plan, and you need to do your homework. Under the federal SECURE Act, which went into effect January 1, 2020, for example, Roth IRAs have become especially attractive for many people. In a Roth, you pay taxes on money going into your account and then all future withdrawals are tax free. That changes the internal investment strategy a good deal.

Overall, the goal for you and your heirs is simple:

Leave the money in as long as possible, but don't create a tax trap for the future.

## TAX BRACKET ARBITRAGE

Let's call the overall game "tax bracket arbitrage." Anyone with significant IRA assets must learn this game. Don't like to play games? You will certainly lose out and probably court disaster.

As of this writing, there are seven federal income tax brackets, with rates of 10%, 12%, 22%, 24%, 32%, 35%, and 37%. It's a big deal jumping from one to the next. The higher your income in a given year, the higher percentage of your income must be paid in taxes. Someone who makes $1 million a year pays a higher percentage than a person who makes $100,000 a year.

When you pull money from a traditional IRA, it adds to your income for that year. So exactly when you withdraw IRA money, stretch out IRA money, or convert IRA money to a

Roth IRA will be crucial to your financial well-being. This game makes it possible to double your money, triple your money, *or lose half or more* to *taxes and penalties,* depending on your timing, your math, your memory for deadlines, and your arbitrage skills.

You need professional help, but you have to understand the situation well enough to get the right kind of help and check their work.

## IRAS HAVE BECOME A BIG, BIG DEAL

In the beginning, nobody really thought an IRA would be a significant wealth creator. It was supposed to be a substitute for defined benefit plans like pensions, in which you get your $3,000 or $5,000 a month after you retire, guaranteed.

But IRAs and the like quickly became major investment pathways. Accounts grew to hundreds of thousands if not millions of dollars.

During the 2012 election campaign, we learned that Mitt Romney had about $100 million in his retirement account. More recently, we hear that Peter Thiel's Roth IRA is over $5 billion! Will money be left in those accounts for the kids when these folks pass away? One would assume. Will their kids handle the payouts correctly and avoid stupid mistakes? Don't assume so at all.

## PAINFUL COMPLEXITY

ERISA first launched in 1974, but it's been amended many times. Rarely have those amendments made the subject any simpler. By now, the subject has become so complex, it makes many people's eyes hurt, even mine—and I'm an expert!

The changes that became effective on January 1, 2020 with the federal SECURE Act were especially profound.

Ironically, it was an attempt to *simplify* the situation. It did not.

The SECURE Act, which stands for "Setting Every Community Up for Retirement Enhancement," requires *everyone* to launch a review of their IRA planning, because now there's even more you don't know you don't know.

In fact, because no one advisor *ever* understands how this all works, I strongly suggest that if you have significant IRA assets, you create an "A-Team" led by your lawyer, along with a financial advisor and a CPA—in that order. No single one of these disciplines seems to have the full picture.

As this chapter goes on, we'll look at the serious consequences of estate plans structured *without* an up-to-date understanding of IRAs. That includes *most* estate plans.

## THE OPEN SECRET

Let me start with an open secret that somehow remains a secret.

Your living trust has nothing to do with your IRA, your 401(k), your 403(b), your TSA, or any number of similar vehicles. Your living trust, on its own, does not determine who inherits your IRA.

Neither does a will.

What determines who inherits these monies is the *beneficiary designation on file for each account at each institution.* It *only* matters what's written in the file held by the company administering your IRA, 401(k), or similar account.

It's crucial for you to know that this information will *not* be overridden by your will or trust. You cannot simply rewrite a will or trust and hold on to that piece of paper, thinking you have made a change to your IRA beneficiaries. The change must be made to the file at the institution that holds your account.

It's shocking to me how many estate planning attorneys do not know this simple and crucial fact. Why not? Because it's not the kind of thing taught in law school, and they may not have worked on the back end of estates, administering trusts and solving problems after a death. That said, even expert probate and conservatorship lawyers sometimes make this mistake.

Other kinds of assets, such as life insurance policies and annuities, also have beneficiaries designated at the institutional level, outside of trusts or wills.

To make a change, you must go to each and every institution and make a change to a document with your signature, sometimes witnessed and notarized. These assets generally aren't put into a living trust, because serious negative income tax consequences are likely to occur.

Let me repeat that. Your IRA does not go into your living trust. Your annuities generally should not go into your living trust. Your life insurance generally should not go into your living trust while you are alive.

In the case of an IRA, it may well make sense for you to create a new kind of vehicle, what I call an IRA Legacy Trust, to receive your IRA *after* you die. But if so, that trust will be entirely separate from your living trust, with its own trustee.

We'll talk about IRA Legacy Trusts a bit later, when we get into maximizing the magic of tax deferral. For now, just remember that your retirement and insurance accounts have their own separate life, apart from your living trust.

## IRAS, INSURANCE, AND ANNUITIES ARE *NOT* GENERALLY DISTRIBUTED BY TRUSTEES OR EXECUTORS: EACH HEIR WILL BE ON THEIR OWN

Because IRAs, annuities, and life insurance policies generally exist outside of living trusts, follow the separate laws of contract and not probate, and are controlled by rules at the institutions holding them, *the distribution of such assets is most often not controlled by a trustee or the executor of a will.*

Indeed, as we learned in Mistake #7, trustees and executors (often the same person), have no legal responsibility to see that such assets are distributed to beneficiaries *at all.* Institutions will usually not even talk to the executor or a successor trustee, only the named beneficiaries. They won't give a mere executor the time of day.

Equally important, the laws applying to a particular asset with a beneficiary designation will not be controlled by the laws in your state but *the laws of the state in which the assets are held.*

This fact creates both problems and opportunities, which we will also discuss further on. But for now, know that when it comes to IRAs, other ERISA plans, insurance, annuities, and similar assets controlled not by living trusts but by beneficiary designations at the institutional level, *all beneficiaries will be on their own once you die.*

That means one or all of these beneficiaries are likely to

make some huge mistakes. And if a beneficiary listed on an asset has already died, a legal mess may well ensue. Indeed, the institution may end up never having to distribute the money at all—a frequent occurrence.

## IRA WITHDRAWALS DURING YOUR LIFETIME

Before we get to the surprising problems and opportunities your heirs will face with your IRA, I want to talk about *you*.

This is an estate planning book, but seriously, most people significantly screw up their IRA opportunities during their own lifetimes, limiting their own retirements. Let me spend just a little time in the hope of educating you and preventing you from making the most common mistakes. It will also help you understand the problem faced by your heirs.

The basic rules are these:

1. Understand the rules; they are complicated.
2. Carefully plan your contributions and withdrawals to avoid massive penalties and minimize taxes.
3. Get expert advice; this is not a DIY project.

### BIRTHDAYS MATTER, A LOT

In order to get the maximum benefit from IRAs and avoid

catastrophic tax situations, you need to understand not just how traditional IRAs work as people age, but how they work for different parties to an estate.

Everyone's birthdays and their related withdrawal deadlines are crucial to proper IRA management, not just for heirs, but for the original owners of an IRA. Original owners, surviving spouses, and other beneficiaries all face significantly different rules. There are also special circumstances for minor children under the age of 18 (and in school up to age 26); people with disabilities or chronic illness; spouses; cases when the original owner of the IRA is less than ten years older than the inheritor of the IRA; and when the original owner has already started "required minimum distributions"—now at age 72.

In other words: complicated. Reading this chapter will help you understand what you don't know, but it will not make you an expert.

The *Participant* is what the IRS calls the "original owner" of an IRA (I use both terms interchangeably). Under current rules, as a Participant, you can start taking money out without a tax penalty at age 59 1/2, but you absolutely must start taking money out of your own IRA (or other ERISA account) no later than April 1 following the year in which you turn 72. (That's if you were born after July 1, 1949. Otherwise, it's the April 1 following the year in which you turn 70 1/2.)

When you die, your heirs must start taking money out the year after your death.

Not surprisingly, many people have never heard of this deadline, or they become confused, or otherwise miss the proper withdrawal date, triggering serious long-term tax consequences and huge penalties. For those who have passed the deadline, it may be burned into their memories.

April 1 following the year you turn 72 is your Required Beginning Date, or RBD for withdrawals from a traditional IRA. If you are 72 before December 31 of a given year, then the following April 1, you have to take out at least 3.6496350% of your IRA funds.

This is called your Required Minimum Distribution (RMD). It comes around every year, and it changes every year—though after your first RMD, you no longer get the grace period until April 1; you have to do it by December 31 each year.

## CALCULATING YOUR ALL-IMPORTANT RMDS

If you're Mitt Romney with a $100 million traditional IRA, your first RMD is $3,649,635.00. If you are a normal person with a $100,000 IRA, you have to remove at least $3,649.64. If you are a rich-normal person with a $1 million IRA, it's $36,496.35 by April 1. The money goes from the left pocket to the right pocket, *and you pay tax.*

After that, you have to keep removing money according to something called the Uniform Table for Determining Factor Lifetime Distributions. Each year, you have to take a different Required Minimum Distribution, the annual RMD.

Below, we reproduce the updated Uniform Lifetime Table for 2022. You need to check each year to see if this table has been revised. Also check our webpage where we post updates to this book, at www.cunninghamlegal.com/savvybook.

### UNIFORM LIFETIME TABLE*

For use by unmarried owners, married owners whose spouses are not more than 10 years younger, and married owners whose spouses are not sole beneficiaries of their IRAs (others must use different tables)

| Age | Uniform Table RMD Factor | Age | Uniform Table RMD Factor | Age | Uniform Table RMD Factor |
|---|---|---|---|---|---|
| 72 | 27.4 | 89 | 12.9 | 105 | 4.6 |
| 73 | 26.5 | 90 | 12.2 | 106 | 4.3 |
| 74 | 25.5 | 91 | 11.5 | 107 | 4.1 |
| 75 | 24.6 | 92 | 10.8 | 108 | 3.9 |
| 76 | 23.7 | 93 | 10.1 | 109 | 3.7 |
| 77 | 22.9 | 94 | 9.5 | 110 | 3.5 |
| 78 | 22.0 | 95 | 8.9 | 111 | 3.4 |
| 79 | 21.1 | 96 | 8.4 | 112 | 3.3 |
| 80 | 20.2 | 97 | 7.8 | 113 | 3.1 |
| 81 | 19.4 | 98 | 7.3 | 114 | 3.0 |
| 82 | 18.5 | 99 | 6.8 | 115 | 2.9 |
| 83 | 17.7 | 100 | 6.4 | 116 | 2.8 |
| 84 | 16.8 | 101 | 6.0 | 117 | 2.7 |
| 85 | 16.0 | 102 | 5.6 | 118 | 2.5 |
| 86 | 15.2 | 103 | 5.2 | 119 | 2.3 |
| 87 | 14.4 | 104 | 4.9 | 120+ | 2.0 |
| 88 | 13.7 | | | | |

* Effective January 1, 2022

You absolutely need to learn how to use this table and how we derived that 3.6496350% so you can do the math for yourself every year. Your heirs have to learn their own table, which is different.

Here goes: we got the 3.6496350% by looking at the table under age 72 (the first distribution, or RBD), and seeing "27.4" listed.

When we divided 1 by 27.4, we got 3.6496350%. There is no rounding up or down. That means you have to take out a minimum of 3.6496350% by April 1 of the year following the year in which you turn 72.

After your first distribution, in each following year, you have to take out a certain percentage of your remaining funds by December 31, based on the age you will turn by December 31 of that same year. No grace period. Accounts are valued, for distribution purposes, on December 31 of the year prior to the distribution.

So, if you turn 80 anytime during a given year, you look at the chart and see "20.2" next to 80. That means you take 1 divided by 20.2 and get 4.9504950%. You have to withdraw at least 4.9504950% of the value of the prior December 31 by December 31 of the year of distribution.

Clear as mud.

As you can see, the Uniform Lifetime Table starts at 72 and goes up to age 120+. Chances are, you will have pulled out all your IRA money by age 120. Oddly, if you *only* pull out your minimum distribution, you will be living Zeno's Paradox and *never* fully deplete your IRA. Even at age 120 and higher, you are only required to take out 50% of your remaining funds.

*Make sure you and your heirs find and use the right table: the tables are different for different groups, including beneficiaries and minors.*

## HUGE PENALTIES FOR MISSING RMD DEADLINES

If you fail to take the first Required Minimum Distribution (RMD) on your Required Beginning Date (RBD), the government imposes an excise tax of 50% of the amount that should have been withdrawn from your traditional IRA.

Seriously. A 50% penalty!

If you have a $1 million IRA, and you were supposed to take out $36,496.35, your tax penalty will be $18,248.18. That's money thrown away. Gone. Just for missing a deadline.

Importantly, during the pandemic year of 2020, the government suspended most RMDs on IRAs. That may have created a trap for many, as it may confuse beginning dates and get people out of the rhythm of making their RMDs. Be aware.

You may have also heard of an additional penalty called the Five-Year Rule, but that applies to inherited IRAs. We'll learn more about that particular trap later on.

## THE TRULY SPECIAL MAGIC OF ROTH IRAS

In my professional experience, not enough people give Roth IRAs the attention that they deserve. Roth IRAs are *very* different from "regular" or "traditional" IRAs, and often a far superior way of handling retirement funds. Among their wonderful qualities: no RMDs, and no worries about RMD penalties for you.

You need to start thinking Roth. Indeed, because of changes that came with the SECURE Act, creating a Roth or converting a regular IRA to a Roth has become the *single most powerful financial planning tool you have to deal with your IRAs*. Here's the basic picture:

1. As in a regular IRA, you only contribute earned income to a Roth.
2. Unlike in a regular IRA, you have to pay taxes before you deposit your money into the account.

But here's the special Roth magic:

3. No matter how much your money grows in a Roth IRA account, you *never* have to pay any more taxes on that money. And unless you are wealthy enough to trigger an estate tax, *neither do the people who inherit your Roth.*
4. You also *never* have to take any minimum annual distributions throughout your entire life the way you have to with a regular IRA.

With a Roth, you skip all that RMD and Lifetime Table stuff while you are alive, along with the crazy penalties. You can just withdraw money whenever you need it.

## BUT KNOW THE ROTH RULES AND POTENTIAL DOWNSIDES

As with regular, traditional IRAs, there are plenty of rules that I can't cover here, and of course potential downsides.

Most importantly, Roths are a *long-term play only.* They only make sense if you can hang on to the money a long time, so you make up for the tax hit and avoid early-withdrawal penalties.

Indeed, with a Roth, you have to wait to take any withdrawals until five years after January 1 of the year in which you make your contribution, and you must be over 59 1/2. Otherwise, there's a 10% penalty.

Do your homework, and get a pro before you leap.

## THE IMPORTANCE OF ROTHS FOR YOUR HEIRS

We haven't yet spoken about the amazing opportunities and potential disasters you may create for the people who inherit your IRA accounts. At this point, however, I need to say that if you create a Roth IRA or convert your existing IRA to a Roth, you will be doing your heirs a huge favor.

Though most people who inherit a Roth IRA will have to take RMDs from the inherited Roth, they won't have to pay income taxes on those RMDs, and they will be protected from future tax rate increases.

Roths also partly compensate for the loss of lifetime stretches on many inherited IRAs created after the SECURE Act, which imposed a 10-year withdrawal period for inherited IRAs on most categories of heirs.

We'll learn more when we get to our discussion of inherited IRAs.

## MORE MAGIC: ROTH CONVERSIONS

Maybe you're starting to get excited about Roths, but you already have a lot of money in a traditional IRA. You will be happy to hear that you can actually *convert* your traditional IRA to a Roth.

The conversion is not difficult, but you absolutely must

do it through your "A-Team" of reliable experts, and you need to be aware of potential pitfalls. You certainly need to follow more rules than I can cover here. I'll just give you a taste:

1. You will have to pay tax on the full amount of the conversion, so you need to time any conversions carefully (typically in smaller chunks each year)—ideally when both your income and the market dips.
2. You can't withdraw any money from your Roth IRA for five years after the conversion without penalties.
3. There are other complex rules to learn, including the order in which money is withdrawn from your retirement accounts.

Deciding to do any conversion is *not* a no-brainer. For example:

4. A conversion might be a bad idea if you have high income now and expect to have low income later.
5. Maybe you just can't afford to pay the taxes for the conversion *and* wait five years before making further withdrawals.

## USUALLY PARTIAL AND INCREMENTAL

Although some people do a lump-sum conversion to a Roth, most conversions are partial and completed in small increments over a period of years—perhaps 5%, 10% or 15% of your IRA funds each year—because of tax bracket consequences.

You will encounter plenty of other strategic issues: for example, it's generally best to convert before age 72, while remembering that you have to wait 5 years before the first withdrawal. And then, of course, you need to think about your overall investment balancing act: just what will go into your Roth as opposed to your other accounts?

Again, not a DIY project.

Earlier, I mentioned Peter Thiel. I love to tell the full story: Thiel was a PayPal founder who converted a $2,000 traditional IRA to a Self-Directed Roth (yes, they exist), invested it early in PayPal, then in "The Facebook" when it was valued at a mere $5 million, and now has that $5 *billion* Roth IRA on which he—and his heirs—will *never* have to pay any income tax.

Yes, there will likely be a substantial Death Tax, and your own results may vary. But still...

## CREATING THREE POSSIBLE DOORWAYS FOR HEIRS

Now that you have a basic understanding of IRAs, RBDs, and RMDs, we're finally ready to get to IRA estate planning.

Unless you actively hate your heirs, do not say, "Well, I'll be dead; they'll have to figure this out for themselves." If you do this, you will practically guarantee an IRA disaster for them.

You created the IRA. It's *your* responsibility to understand the opportunities and pitfalls, plan accordingly, and find a way to pass that knowledge on.

Why must your heirs also have a deep understanding? *The rules for inherited IRAs are very different than the rules for original Participants.* But like you, heirs must take precise, positive actions on your carefully nurtured IRA and step through the proper doors at the proper moments.

Your decisions create those doors. I call them: 1. The Door to Disasters; 2. The Door to Missed Opportunities; and 3. The Door to Successful Outcomes.

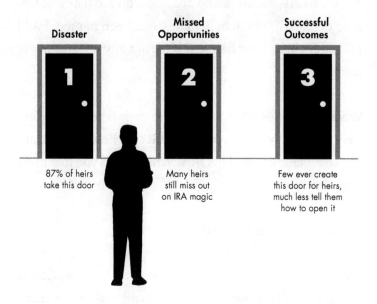

## YOUR IRA HEIR WILL STEP THROUGH
## ONE OF THESE DOORS

| Disaster | Missed Opportunities | Successful Outcomes |
|---|---|---|
| **1** | **2** | **3** |
| 87% of heirs take this door | Many heirs still miss out on IRA magic | Few ever create this door for heirs, much less tell them how to open it |

## DOOR # 1: PHIL GETS DAD'S IRA AND A DISASTER

Let's take a look at the all-too-common case of Phil, who, like 87% of all heirs, steps through the IRA Door to Disasters. We'll keep it simple.

Phil's mom is gone. His dad built up a wonderful $200,000 IRA, and he designated his only child, Phil, as the beneficiary of the account upon his death.

When Phil's dad dies on Christmas Day, Phil has a lot to deal with, but accessing the IRA proves surprisingly easy. All he has to do is show up at his dad's investment company with the death certificate and his own photo ID. Unlike most other asset types, there's no probate required if a clear Payable on Death (POD) beneficiary has been named. We'll talk later about what happens if there's any uncertainty in the POD.

When Phil stands at the front desk in early January, the clerk says, "I'm sorry about your father. It says here that you are the sole beneficiary of his IRA. What would you like to do with the account?"

Phil blinks, and asks, "Do?"

"Well," says the clerk. "You have several options. One is to just take all the money out now. I can write you a check today if you like."

"Okay," says Phil, who would really love to have $200,000 in his pocket right now. And who wouldn't? "I'll take that option."

Now, as I will repeat throughout this book, about half of everyone who inherits money blows it right away. They do this because they don't have a clue about the real-world consequences of their actions. Let's see how it plays out for Phil.

"No problem," says the clerk. "I'll just need your Social Security number."

"Why?" asks Phil.

"Well, if you don't give it to us, we have to keep 24%. If you give us your Social Security number, then we withhold 10% for taxes...or whatever amount you tell us to withhold."

"Fantastic," says Phil. "Here's my Social Security number. I'll take my check for $180,000. You hold on to the $20,000 that goes to the government. Cut my check!"

Ten minutes later, Phil has a check for $180,000 in his pocket. He's a bit more responsible than Jane's husband in Mistake #6. He doesn't go out and buy a bass boat, but he does add a second story to his house, he upgrades his car, and he sends his kid off to a private college. Six months later, the money's gone. The $20,000 already covered the taxes, right?

Wrong.

### TWELVE MONTHS LATER COMES THE HIT

Come the following January, Phil gets a 1099-R in the mail from the bank that held Phil's dad's IRA. If Phil ignores that

1099-R and doesn't report the payout to the IRS, he's going to get in big trouble. The IRS is going to come after him.

But let's say Phil is a responsible taxpayer, and he takes his 1099-R for $200,000 to the accountant who prepares his tax returns.

"Wow," says the accountant. "I didn't know about this IRA distribution. You've just added $200,000 to your income for last year. That's going to kick you into a much higher tax bracket."

Unless he has a whole lot of other deductions, Phil might now owe $50,000, $70,000, or even $100,000 to the government on that $200,000 he pulled out of the IRA. In any case, it's highly unlikely that the $20,000 withheld by the investment company will cover the bill. The minimum withholding is almost never enough.

Say Phil needs to come up with an additional *$60,000 beyond the $20,000 already withheld*—not an unusual result. Where will he get it? Remember, he already spent the $200,000 months ago.

Now he's in serious debt to the IRS, which has been waiting all this time to collect the taxes deferred by Phil's father. Well, that time has come.

Is this a common situation? Yes, I see it happen every day.

Like I said, a full 87 percent of heirs withdraw the IRA funds immediately, heedless of the consequences, and many get into situations equally this bad.

Will yours?

## THREE CLASSES OF BENEFICIARIES

Now that we see one of the disasters that can await your unwitting IRA heirs, let's step back and understand how inherited IRAs work overall. Otherwise, you won't understand the other possible disasters and opportunities.

The first thing you have to know is that the rules for inherited IRAs are significantly different for different kinds of heirs. And in every case, the rules are *not* the same as for you, the original Participant. It's your job to set up your estate so your IRAs work for all these people, in their own way.

Complicated, but doable.

Here are the three general classes of people who may inherit your IRA, assuming you took the trouble to specifically designate them as beneficiaries at the institution holding your IRA.

Note: These rules apply to all deaths January 1, 2020 and later. If you are the heir to a person who died December 31, 2019 and earlier, different rules apply, and you must learn them. In any case, this chapter does not give a comprehensive look at the complex tax rules for inherited IRAs. Get a savvy, expert CPA or lawyer to help you.

## CLASS 1: SPOUSES

Spouses have a huge advantage on IRAs. A spouse can simply roll over a deceased spouse's IRA into their own IRA account. In most cases, a rollover will be the right thing to do if the surviving spouse is over 59 1/2, but a lawyer, CPA, and financial advisor should be consulted on other options that may be better in certain situations too complex to detail here (such as when a spouse is under 59 1/2).

If your spouse rolls over an IRA, they must follow all the same rules about RMDs that you had to follow, on their own age schedule, using their own proper Lifetime Table. Like you, if they follow the rules and don't miss any deadlines, they will be able to stretch the IRA out over their entire lifetime.

This assumes, of course, that your spouse knows all the rules and is prepared to act. What are the odds that he or she will do the homework, hit the deadlines, use the right table, not incur dreadful penalties, and remember to do tax bracket arbitrage?

Remember also that the definition of "spouse" may vary greatly by state and may be different at the federal level. As I write, for example, here in California, the terms "registered domestic partner" and "spouse" are interchangeable under *California law*, but that is *not true for the feds*. You may be able to file a joint return in California, but you cannot act like a spouse to roll over an IRA. These definitions are in constant flux, and you absolutely have to find out before you take action.

Does your spouse understand all this?

## CLASS 2: "ELIGIBLE DESIGNATED BENEFICIARIES"

Certain people, called Eligible Designated Beneficiaries (or EDBs), can also stretch out the withdrawals from their inherited IRAs over their IRS-defined projected lifetimes, although they cannot do a simple rollover.

Let me repeat: spouses are the only heirs with the rollover privilege. If you were not married to the person who died, you cannot roll over the IRA into your own IRA, ever. People make this mistake all the time.

Under current law, the larger Eligible Designated Beneficiary class *only* includes: a disabled or chronically ill individual; any individual who is not more than 10 years younger than you; and your own minor children. The situation for minor children can be complex. In most cases, they must withdraw all the money within 10 years of their 18th birthday, while following the RMD rules during those 10 years. In some states, "minor child" may include full-time students up to the age of 26.

In other words, this class does not include most of your adult children or grandchildren. Most will fall into Class 3, below.

Eligible Designated Beneficiaries who inherit your IRA must quickly begin taking Required Minimum Distributions (RMDs), but they use a different table to calculate the RMD for each year, called the "Single Life Table," published by the IRS. If they screw up, they will face significant tax penalties, with the addition of the dreaded Five-Year Rule, which I detail below.

Will your younger sister or the guardian of your disabled child take the trouble to understand all this?

## CLASS 3: REGULAR "DESIGNATED BENEFICIARIES" AND THE TEN-YEAR RULE

Ninety percent or more of the people who will inherit your IRA, and who are not your surviving spouse, will likely be considered regular, non-eligible "Designated Beneficiaries." These are the people you properly designated on your

IRA account paperwork at your custodian institution, *not* in your living trust.

Under the SECURE Act, these folks can *no longer* stretch IRA distributions over their lifetimes. They need not take RMDs, but they must follow what I call the Ten-Year Rule.

While it eliminated the advantages of stretched-out IRAs, the Ten-Year Rule was intended to simplify IRA inheritances. Actually, it made IRA planning more difficult and possibly more prone to disaster for most.

Generally speaking, a regular Designated Beneficiary may take out as much money as they wish as quickly as they wish—though as we saw in the case of Phil, "quickly" is often a very bad idea. But in the tenth year (which is actually the eleventh *tax* year), *all* the money must come out by December 31 of the year that contains the tenth anniversary of death. Not a happy anniversary on many levels—death *and* taxes.

### WHAT IF NO WITHDRAWAL OCCURS IN THE TENTH YEAR?

Now let's look a little more closely at that "Ten-Year Rule" deadline—and remember, this applies only to inherited IRAs and only to *non-Eligible, but Designated Beneficiaries* on your IRA account paperwork.

Under the Ten-Year Rule, a Designated Beneficiary can do the following:

1. Pull all the money out at once. This will almost certainly create a disaster. See Phil and Door #1, above.
2. Take the money out over a term of ten years in a carefully measured way so as not to push any one year into a higher tax bracket—with everything out by the end of the year that contains the tenth anniversary of death. This could work out fairly well—or not. It all depends on the level of tax bracket arbitrage the heir manages to exercise as well as the performance of the investments in the IRA.
3. Wait until the last minute and pull out all the money right before the 10-Year deadline. This will also likely create a tax disaster.

If the ten-year deadline slips by and your heir simply forgets to withdraw all the IRA money, guess what? The IRS will impose an excise tax of 50 percent.

Got that? Fifty percent of all the money left!

If your IRA has grown to $1 million, that's a $500,000 excise tax. I guarantee that if your heir makes this mistake, it will make you turn over in your grave, even though you've been underground for 10+ years.

As this book goes to print, the new rule is still pretty recent, so it will be a long time before we know how many heirs will make this catastrophic mistake. Based on my experience, however, I guarantee the number will be large.

## DISASTERS IF HEIRS FAIL TO RAPIDLY NAIL DOWN THEIR STATUS

You and your heirs need to know that there's nothing automatic about becoming either a Designated Beneficiary or an Eligible Designated Beneficiary.

You yourself have to take steps while you are alive. Then, when you die, they have to quickly take steps too. Otherwise, tax disasters *will* occur.

As I mentioned, you have to clearly indicate your PODs (Payable on Death beneficiaries) at your financial institution, and you have to carefully update those designations when new heirs are born, when heirs die or change their names, or when other major life changes occur.

Fail to keep it all updated? Disaster.

*When you die, your heirs* must also take direct action. Eligible Designated Beneficiaries, known as EDBs, must do a bunch of stuff in a timely manner, *or they will lose their eligible status* and wake up to a tax nightmare.

For starters, every Designated Beneficiary and Eligible Beneficiary must clearly identify themselves to the custodian institution by September 30 of the year following your death. If you die in December, that's not a whole lot of time. When they (or their custodian) finally get over to your bank or your brokerage, proving their status will prove problematic if you were not really careful with your part of the job. That means you recorded and updated their specific names, name changes, dates of birth, and Social Security numbers, and you specified the right rules about their potential children, or "issue." This is especially problematic when a *beneficiary* dies without the PODs being updated; without clear rules about the next in line, legal confusion can ensue.

If a trust is a beneficiary of the IRA, a copy of the trust must be delivered to the custodian for the IRA no later than October 31 of the year following death—what we call the Halloween Rule.

Eligible Designated Beneficiaries must take their first distribution by December 31 of the year following your death (their Required Beginning Date, or RBD). Again, if your heir has died, and the new heir is the "issue" of your named beneficiary, this may be especially problematic.

As we saw above, the big trap for regular Designated Beneficiaries is thinking "I don't have to do anything for 10 years," then either experiencing a massive tax hit in that

10th year or forgetting the deadline and losing 50% of the money in penalties.

## DISASTER IS CERTAIN IF HEIRS DON'T KNOW ABOUT YOUR IRA

Even if you've taken the trouble to make a living trust and a will, your heirs may not even be aware of your IRA—a frequent occurrence. After all, if you have a trust, it's not in the trust. If it's in your will, your trustee is not responsible for disbursing it and may not keep everyone apprised of the issues. It might be in another state, where you rolled over your 401(k) twenty years ago.

Given all these challenges, how likely is it your heirs will hit the above deadlines?

If your brother Bob is handling all this after you die, does he have the dates of birth of all your beneficiaries? Their Social Security numbers? Will he worry about stuff that's not in your living trust?

## DISASTERS CAN OCCUR FOR MINORS TOO

Minors, people with disabilities, and the chronically ill (essentially unable to work due to illness) are at a special disadvantage when it comes to hitting the deadlines.

To get their Eligible status, even a two-year-old needs her

guardian to take these actions by September 30, Halloween, and December 31 of the year following your death.

If the guardian doesn't know about the deadlines, the child may well lose all the advantages of stretching out IRA distributions. She will be stuck with the Five-Year Rule below and be required to withdraw her money by age seven.

In any case, as mentioned above, most minor children must take all their distributions within 10 years of reaching age 18. How many people in their early twenties will do the right kind of tax and investment planning to do that properly? How many will simply pull out all the money at once, with a gigantic tax hit?

### A POTENTIAL FIVE-YEAR PENALTY DISASTER FOR ELIGIBLE HEIRS

If your Eligible heirs blow *anything* in the above—such as failing to identify themselves in time or missing an RMD—they will likely be stuck with the "Five-Year Rule" if you haven't reached your RBD, or they will be stuck with your remaining life expectancy if you have reached your RBD. Or worse.

Under the Five-Year Rule, your Eligible heirs can no longer stretch IRA distributions out over their lifetimes. They will be forced to take the money out in five substantially equal payments over just five years.

This could easily cut their overall IRA income by a third, a half, or much more compared to what they could have made by stretching their IRA as long as possible.

This penalty has become so common that many people think the Five-Year Rule is just the normal way for Eligible Beneficiaries to withdraw funds from an inherited IRA. *It's not.* The Five-Year Rule is actually a terrible penalty box.

If you have a person with disabilities, or a chronically ill person inheriting, this mistake will prove especially sad, as it will greatly limit potential financial support which might have lasted their entire lives. A sudden windfall could also throw the loved one with special needs off of public assistance—for more on that, see "Accumulation Trusts" below.

### LIVING TRUSTS OFTEN LEAD TO IRA DISASTERS

Plenty of other common mistakes can lead an heir through Door #1 to disasters or at best, through Door #2 to missed opportunities.

For example, if you foolishly designated your living trust as the beneficiary of your IRA, it's theoretically possible your heirs will still get the benefits of the Ten-Year Rule or maintain their Eligible status—*but in the real world, probably not.*

The reasons are somewhat arcane, but a trust must meet

unusual requirements to qualify as a beneficiary. One of these is brutal: the trust has to be *irrevocable,* meaning you cannot change or amend it, ever.

Most living trusts are revocable for good reason—you will probably make lots of changes to it before you die. The laws will shift. You will want to change beneficiaries for births, deaths, divorces. You will want to add charities.

If you designate your living trust as a beneficiary to your IRA, and right before you die, you do a handwritten amendment saying, "I give my church 1 percent of my estate when I die," that may well blow the whole IRA plan for your heirs. Likely they will all fall under the Five-Year Rule and won't get their designated status.

Now, a lawyer may tell you otherwise. A lawyer may tell you, "Oh, don't worry. A living trust is fine as a beneficiary if you do X, Y, or Z." *Maybe.* But a whole lot of careful planning has to go into that "if," and it's likely to blow up when you're dead.

Don't do it.

## OLD-STYLE CONDUIT TRUSTS BECOME DISASTERS

For many years, clever lawyers have been constructing what are called "conduit trusts" for their clients. Conduits force mandatory distributions at certain times, directly to individuals. They were intended to protect an inherited IRA from creditors such as divorcing spouses, or to protect heirs who might be irresponsible if they got the money under their own control. Conduits were a good idea, but they always had their limitations.

Under the SECURE Act, conduit trusts create a recipe for total disaster.

Say that Phil inherits a $1 million IRA with conduit distributions of $35,000 a year. Phil's dad set this up because he didn't trust Phil not to blow the IRA right off the bat, and he was worried that Phil's wife might want to cash in during a divorce.

Clever idea, but then the SECURE Act came along. Now because Phil is just a Designated Beneficiary (and not an Eligible Designated Beneficiary), Phil has *no RMD* in years one to nine, but in the year that contains the tenth anniversary of his dad's death, the trustee will distribute the *entire IRA* to Phil because that is how the new "minimum distribution" rules work. That's right; Phil is forced to take the *entire* balance of the IRA in one year, with catastrophic tax implications at the very same time he loses the creditor protection offered by the trust! He can only sit around and look for that horrific tax bill and potential conflict with his ex-wife ten years later. If the conduit trust has multiple designated beneficiaries, multiple other messes will occur.

Bottom line: If you have a conduit trust, you *must* consider a redo immediately. You must fix it *now*, before you die and leave your heirs a disaster.

Instead, consider an IRA Legacy Trust, which I discuss later in this chapter.

## DOOR #2: MISSED OPPORTUNITIES

Earlier, we saw Phil walk through Door #1 because like 87 percent of heirs, he and his dad were ignorant of the tax laws around IRAs. We also saw plenty of other disasters lurking behind Door #1. But what if at least *some* planning occurs?

Let's say that Phil does a little research and becomes one of the 13 percent of people who don't yank all the money out of his parents' retirement accounts in year one. He sees that under the SECURE Act, he can space out his withdrawals up until December 31 of the year of the tenth anniversary of his dad's death.

Of course, his options are somewhat limited because his dad didn't do any *serious* planning, like converting to a Roth or creating an IRA Legacy Trust (to be discussed below). And Phil himself doesn't really grasp tax bracket arbitrage.

But our hero does realize—hopefully with a shock—that come that tenth year, he'd better not be forced to take an enormous withdrawal that will throw him into a higher tax bracket. And he'd better not forget to pull it all out before the tenth year drifts by. He also becomes dimly aware that he should be planning his significant withdrawals for when he has low-income years.

As a result, when he walks through Door #2, Phil doesn't walk into a disaster. But without more significant planning, he will still miss out on some huge IRA opportunities. If Phil were disabled or chronically ill, some of these missed opportunities might be truly tragic.

In a table a few pages on, I lay out some possible scenarios for Phil if he walks through Doors 1, 2, or 3. Like many, he will think he did *pretty well* when he walks through Door #2, when he could have done *pretty great* through Door #3.

Look at that chart coming up below, but I could summarize the numbers like this: If Phil and his dad do no planning on that $1 million IRA, Phil ends up with around $500,000. If they do just a teensy bit of planning, Phil gets about $1 million. But if they do some serious planning, Phil steps through Door #3 and likely scores over $2 million!

## DOOR #3: SUCCESSFUL OUTCOMES

Let's say Phil's dad was a smart guy.

Let's say he regularly consulted with his attorney, his financial advisor, and his CPA. In fact, these advisors knew each other so well they had each other's cell numbers. Year after year, they worked together as a team to create a great retirement for Phil's dad, and a great legacy for Phil.

Working with his advisor, Phil's dad got in the habit of annual, bite-sized conversions from his traditional IRA to a Roth IRA. He considered the payment of income taxes in the annual conversion process a wise investment overall.

He also kept Phil aware of the situation and the planning, so Phil's actual life circumstances were properly taken into account—and so he could make the right moves when his dad passed away.

### PHIL'S DAD CREATES A TRUST WITH A NEVADA TRUSTEE

But there's more: Phil's dad did not name Phil as a direct beneficiary of his traditional and Roth IRAs!

Instead, he used his attorney to create an IRA Legacy Trust (not a living trust!) with a trustee located in Nevada, where there were no state income taxes. When he died, the IRA money went into that trust, not into Phil's hands. That way, even though both he and Phil lived in California, he saved Phil from paying (or, in some cases, delayed him from paying) high California taxes when money came out of funds still in a traditional IRA. In California, those taxes are currently up to 13.3%.

This trust is also designed to protect Phil from predators and creditors and allowed him to do some serious tax planning with a financial advisor.

All in all, over ten years, based on judicious withdrawals, tax payments, and re-investments, the total value of the IRA benefit to Phil doubled in value.

## OTHER SMART MOVES

Depending on his specific circumstances, Phil's dad had other smart moves he could make during his lifetime.

Maybe, instead of just Phil, he had multiple heirs, some of whom were doing pretty well, and some of whom weren't.

Maybe, as a truly high-income individual, he also wanted to make a difference in the world, while still ensuring his own wealth.

If Phil's dad had multiple heirs in very different circumstances, he could have worked with a good attorney to create a special kind of "spray trust" to receive the IRA funds. In this kind of trust, the trustee has discretion to distribute, divide, sprinkle, or "spray" the trust funds among the beneficiaries the way he or she sees fit.

As an example, the spray could substitute Roth trust money for taxable funds that might have gone to high-income heirs in order to reduce their tax liability or to protect them from creditors and predators. A savvy trustee for a high-wealth family could make this work out fairly for everyone while protecting family members as appropriate.

Complicated? Yes. Possibly incredibly advantageous to the whole family? You bet.

To leave a legacy for the world at large while still supporting his own retirement, Phil's dad might also have worked with his planning team to create a charitable trust. We'll learn more about those in the next chapter, Mistake #4.

## LOOKING AT POSSIBLE OUTCOMES

Let's look at some possible outcomes for our friend Phil, depending on which doors his dad created and which doors Phil has the wisdom to walk through. For the sake of argument, the chart below assumes a 7.2% return year to year on investments within the IRA account—not unreasonable, given the history of the stock market and some good financial planning.

Remember that Phil is a Designated Beneficiary, not an Eligible Designated Beneficiary, so he's subject to the Ten-Year Rule.

In each strategy, Phil inherits exactly $1 million in an IRA account when his dad dies—except for the Roth IRA, where taxes were paid out during a conversion to Roth years ago. In the next column, we see the total taxes paid by Phil, depending on how well he and his dad play the game.

We already know about the disaster that waits behind **Door #1** if Phil pulled out all the money on day one.

Under **Door #2**, Phil does okay—he makes planned withdrawals each year, but he tries his best to wait as long as possible to pull out all the money, and he does some minimal tax planning. But he and his dad didn't take all the smart steps needed to maximize his returns. Maybe Phil thinks he did pretty well by the IRA, but he's wrong.

Because look how well Phil could have done if his dad had created **Door #3** and explained to Phil how to use that door effectively! In the best possible scenario, Phil's dad converted all his IRA money to a Roth IRA during his lifetime, created an IRA Legacy Trust, and invested reasonably well. When he dies, Phil's dad manages to leave the money in some decent investments for 10 years, tax free.

Result? A wonderful legacy.

## COMPARING THE DOORS

Possible outcomes for the $1M IRA created by Phil's dad. Assumes a 7.2% annual return, residency in California, and current law under the SECURE Act.

| | | Strategy or Lack Thereof | Starting Point at Dad's Death | Total Taxes Paid by Phil | Approx Net Benefit to Phil |
|---|---|---|---|---|---|
| POSSIBLE DOORS FOR PHIL | DOOR #1: Disaster | Immediate withdrawal, with tax hit | $1,000,000 | $472,000 | $528,000 |
| | DOOR #2: Missed Opportunities (but at least a tiny bit of planning) | Ten years of evenly spaced withdrawals, ignoring tax bracket arbitrage | $1,000,000 | $503,664 | $1,050,920 |
| | DOOR #3: Successful Outcomes (over 10-year window, with creditor protection) | Good: traditional legacy IRA trust sited in Nevada, good tax bracket arbitrage | $1,000,000 | $703,886 | $1,444,650 |
| | | Better: two trusts, one 50% Roth, one 50% traditional sited in Nevada, good arbitrage | $1,000,000 | $351,943 | $1,796,593 |
| | | Best: legacy IRA trust with full Roth conversion by Phil's dad, who pre-invested in taxes. Siting of trust unimportant | $1,000,000 | $0 | $2,148,536 |

## LET'S TALK MORE ABOUT IRA LEGACY TRUSTS

I've mentioned the growing importance of IRA Legacy Trusts several times, and in the table, you can see the difference they might make to Phil. Now that you grasp inherited IRAs, I can explain such trusts more clearly. In my practice, we are shifting more and more to these vehicles, especially after passage of the SECURE Act.

Yes, they are complex. They are also powerful.

Under previous law, what people generally called "IRA stretch trusts" were criticized for being complicated and generally unnecessary because most heirs could stretch distributions over their lifetimes without any kind of trust. You only needed trusts in special circumstances, like for special needs heirs, or to provide creditor protection.

Under the new rules, however, maximizing returns and protecting heirs from taxes requires more aggressive action.

Much more.

### HOW IT WORKS

When you work with an expert lawyer to create an IRA Legacy Trust, you are creating a special bucket to receive the money from your IRA when you die.

This trust is named as the sole IRA beneficiary, with individuals named as beneficiaries of the trust.

Because an IRA Legacy Trust is *irrevocable,* it then takes on a life of its own, entirely separate from you or your living trust. Suddenly, everything in this rugged bucket can be controlled by a trustee such as our hero Phil. Let's summarize the benefits before we get into detail:

- Tax Planning Advantages
- Moving the Situs of the Trust to a State without State Income Tax
- Creditor Protection, Even from Divorcing Spouses
- Supporting Special Needs Heirs, Minors, and Aging Heirs
- Providing Overall Management of Inheritance Chains

### TAX PLANNING ADVANTAGES

Because assets accumulate within this "non-grantor" trust with its own tax ID number, there is more flexibility in using tax-advantaged strategies for things like oil and gas investments, solar tax strategies, opportunity zones, real estate, and low-income housing.

Such strategies may not mean much to the average wage earner, but they could be extremely important to a high-wealth individual, and useful to any IRA over $100,000.

The rules for such maneuvers are complex, and often vary by state, so yes, you need serious experts involved.

## MOVING THE *SITUS* TO AVOID OR DELAY STATE TAX

Perhaps most importantly for tax planning, an IRA Legacy Trust receiving money from a traditional IRA can be created *in another state from your residence*—a state where *state* income taxes are low or nonexistent. An individual heir may live in high-tax California, but their IRA Legacy Trust may have its "situs" in, say, zero-tax Nevada. Some other current options are Tennessee, South Dakota, and Alaska.

Locating a trust in Nevada is a whole lot easier than telling your heir to move to Nevada before they pull out your money. In fact, if your heir did move, their original state would probably hunt them down for the taxes. (This happens. I know a tale about a California Franchise Tax Board investigator dumpster-diving in Las Vegas, looking for someone's receipts. Vegas kicked him out.)

I can't go into all the details of the trust's structure and legal status, but *federal* tax liability for a traditional IRA does arrive for your heir when the money comes out of the trust's traditional IRA account and gets deposited into its bank account. Roths, of course, are already exempt from both state and federal taxation.

As a simple example: Suppose Phil inherits a $1 million IRA, and it becomes $1.5 million over the ten years in the traditional IRA Legacy Trust created by his dad, if you include his re-invested withdrawals. If Phil were to take that money out as a California resident, over the years he would pay around $150,000 or more in California income tax alone.

With the trust located in Nevada, Phil will save—or at least defer—$150,000!

Yes, some states do challenge the legal rulings around this from time to time, but as of this writing, it works in most states.

## LOCATION *ALWAYS* MATTERS TO A TRADITIONAL IRA TRUST

It's important to remember that the *situs* of a traditional IRA trust always matters. A lot.

For example, be aware that if a traditional IRA trust is sited in a high-tax state like California with a California trustee, then all the undistributed income of the trust will be subject to California state income tax when it moves from the IRA account to the trust account, *even though the beneficiaries aren't residents of California.* And of course, for California residents too.

That will be very painful to an unwitting heir living in, say, zero-tax Nevada.

## CREDITOR PROTECTION, EVEN FROM DIVORCING SPOUSES

The creditor protections of an IRA Legacy Trust could be vital to any heir at any level of wealth.

In Mistake #6: Letting Third Parties Take Advantage of Your Beneficiaries, I talked about the importance of setting up your assets in a way that is designed to protect your heirs from unworthy creditors, including divorced spouses. The same issues apply to IRAs.

If you don't take steps to protect an inherited IRA, creditors can sue your heirs to take these assets, too.

In fact, the creditor or predator situation can be even worse with IRAs than with other assets because the act of withdrawing the money from an IRA to pay off creditors will *also* trigger tax payments. As of this writing, the question of who gets stuck with the resulting tax remains unsettled in law. It might well be your heir—a terrible double hit. Imagine your heir losing their IRA to creditors *and* getting stuck with the resulting tax bill!

The IRA Legacy Trust is designed to keep even ex-spouses from going after that money while it is in an irrevocable trust.

## IMPORTANT FOR MINORS, ELDERLY, AND LOVED ONES WITH SPECIAL NEEDS: ACCUMULATION TRUSTS

Do you have an heir who is disabled or has special needs?

For such an heir, it might actually be a catastrophe for them to directly inherit IRA money from you. Why? Because that money could well pull them off of public assistance.

The solution is a type of irrevocable Legacy Trust known as an "IRA Accumulation Trust." Such a trust allows for crucial tax and benefits planning not normally available to individuals.

Basically, in an Accumulation Trust, a trustee is named who does not have to distribute any particular RMDs, even for Eligible Designated Beneficiaries, and can instead allow distributions to accumulate in the trust until they decide to dole out money, in careful increments, to the beneficiary.

Lifelong support can be provided in this manner, not just for special needs beneficiaries but for minor children, or elderly heirs.

## PITFALLS TO ACCUMULATION TRUSTS

Be aware that an uninformed attorney can easily screw up an Accumulation Trust for an otherwise Eligible Designated Beneficiary. Partly, this is because attorneys are more familiar with old "conduit" trusts, which are similar but follow different rules.

Remember that for Eligible Designated Beneficiaries, those expected Lifetime Tables we learned about earlier are crucial. In the old conduit trust, the IRS only looked at the age of the individual. But in an Accumulation Trust, the IRS actually looks at the age of the *next* person in line, after the disabled or minor beneficiary.

If you leave an Accumulation Trust to an eight-year-old son, but the next in line after him is your sixty-year-old brother, your eight-year-old son will lose out on his more favorable Eligible Designated Beneficiary RMDs.

Complicated? You bet. As with all IRA trusts (indeed, all trusts!), do not try this at home.

## IRA LEGACY TRUSTS PROVIDE VITAL MANAGEMENT

Finally, an IRA Legacy Trust offers crucial control over your legacy.

Let's assume you understand about Payable-on-Death accounts (PODs), and you carefully update POD information as your heirs are born, get married, get divorced, contemplate divorce, hit old age, become disabled, become wealthy, or run into bankruptcy. Let's say that they're all later informed enough to hit the deadlines and take the proper withdrawals without a trustee to manage the process after you die.

Doing that management at multiple institutions, with multiple heirs and possibly their children, is truly fraught with peril. The slightest mistake can cause enormous headaches. Never forget that the people who run banks and brokerages are not there to make sure the right people get your money when you die. *The rules are different at every institution, and any delay is in their favor as the holder of your funds. Do not blindly rely on these institutions.*

The uncertainty continues after you die. You have no idea if your heirs will face a divorce or bankruptcy years after you are gone, and they need you to protect that inherited IRA for them now, while you can.

With an IRA Legacy Trust, you create a single ship that you can captain during your lifetime. You then pass on that captaincy to a trustee, just as you will do with your living trust.

With any luck, your Good Ship IRA will sail smoothly onward even after you've left the helm.

### CAN YOU DEPEND SOLELY ON A FINANCIAL ADVISOR?

Since we're talking ships, let's look more closely at captains and crews.

Despite the SECURE Act "simplification," will your heirs need professional help to manage a large IRA? For sure. And depending on their circumstances, a large IRA for some people might be $100,000 or less.

I've already talked about your three-member team of lawyer, financial advisor, and CPA.

But without a doubt, the larger your wealth, the more likely you and your heirs will have a full-on wealth management or financial advisory firm handling your money.

This firm will *probably* get your IRA RMDs right. It will *probably* also remember to help your Designated Beneficiaries pull money out in a reasonable series of withdrawals before their ten-year deadline. It will *probably not,* for example, invest in a long-term CD that will tie the money up beyond a deadline—a mistake many individual heirs will make.

*Maybe* the advisory firm will get it right, but don't count on it. Especially if your heir moves the money from Firm A to Firm B, and the tracking of deadlines gets interrupted. Will a later company even have a way to track back to the year of your death once the account is renamed?

Remember that the primary mission of a wealth advisory firm is to make themselves money, make you money, and help to provide a liquid capital market in the US—in that order.

Somewhere *way* down that list is making sure you follow the rules on your taxes. Indeed, advisory firms are often unbelievably ignorant about tax law and strategies.

Bottom line: you and your heirs will always need to know what you know and what you don't know.

## DON'T MISHANDLE LIFE INSURANCE

Just as IRAs are a complex topic, so is life insurance. Sorry, it's just true.

Just as you should not include IRAs in your living trust, you should also not *automatically* make your living trust the owner or beneficiary of your life insurance policy. At least not without some thought and advice.

As you may know, there are two primary categories of life insurance: "term" and "permanent."

A term policy is in force for a specified period of time and is typically used by younger families. A working father with two kids and nonworking spouse will take out a twenty-year policy to ensure that if anything happens to him, his family won't starve.

In practice, such policies rarely pay out at a death, and most people stop paying on them long before they actually pass away.

Hence, most people with term policies *do* put down their living trust as their insurance beneficiary. In this way, the money will be added to the living trust with all the inherent protections we have discussed before. Any payout money will also be managed along with the trust, so if you have more children, for example, you need only add their names to the trust, not to your policies.

## YOUR CREDITORS MAY GO AFTER AN INSURANCE PAYOUT TO A LIVING TRUST

But there's a big downside to naming your living trust as the beneficiary of your life insurance: in many states, if you owe money before you die, *there's a path for your creditors to get the insurance death benefit from your living trust.*

Say you are the pilot of a small plane, and you die in a crash, taking out others with you. Your estate might be successfully sued by their families to take your life insurance money. No kidding.

Depending on your situation and on your state, and especially with longer-term policies, you may need a different strategy, which might include an irrevocable life insurance trust.

## LARGER, PERMANENT INSURANCE PLANS REQUIRE DIFFERENT APPROACHES

As its name implies, a *permanent* policy (think whole life, universal live, variable life, etc.) is a permanent investment vehicle. It is very different from a term policy. Permanent policies often accumulate "cash value"—savings of sorts— and are often used in buy-sell arrangements among business partners and for financial and estate planning purposes.

If you own the policy at death, the death proceeds on life insurance are considered part of your estate for estate tax purposes, and a large payout can push an heir over the estate tax threshold—forcing your heirs to pay estate taxes to the feds.

Remember that some states also impose an inheritance tax on large estates, in addition to the bite from the IRS.

It's important not to set up a trap for your heirs with your insurance payout—or for yourself—with a big sum of money that may be targeted by creditors or predators. Why? Because depending on the laws in your state, the money accumulated in your permanent policy may be threatened by creditors even during your own lifetime.

## CONSIDER AN IRREVOCABLE LIFE INSURANCE TRUST

If someone with significant means establishes a significant

life insurance policy with a benefit of, let's say, $4 million, they should consider creating a separate, irrevocable "life insurance trust."

This separate, irrevocable trust is both the owner and the beneficiary of the insurance policy. When you die, that money is paid out to the trust, not to the estate. Hence, it will not be part of the "taxable" estate. This money is often then lent to the estate to provide liquidity to pay taxes.

Importantly, money can be protected from both your creditors and your heirs' creditors while it is in this irrevocable trust. Not true in a living trust.

If you wish, you can structure the trust to pay for your life insurance premiums and make additional contributions to it during your lifetime.

## KNOWINGLY OR UNKNOWINGLY SCREWING UP

Before we move to the next chapter, I just have to repeat that *most* people screw up the inheriting of IRAs, life insurance policies, and the like. Usually without knowing it.

Sometimes they knowingly screw up because they get impatient.

I'm sitting in a meeting with the son and daughter-in-law

of a deceased couple. The son has inherited a $1 million IRA that his parents worked a lifetime to accumulate. I tell this couple that if they cash out the IRA right away, they will have to pay a whopping 50 percent tax on the money—$500,000. To my shock, the daughter-in-law says, "That's fine. We're okay with paying the $500,000 in taxes because we want to pay off my Mercedes and the mortgage."

I find this kind of thing heartbreaking. A million dollars is sitting in a bank, but they're in too much of a hurry to use half of it!

I think "What if this man's parents were sitting here? How hard did they work to sock away $1 million? What would they say if they saw their son and daughter-in-law throwing away $500,000?"

Such stories happen regularly in my world. Indeed, I have read that even if people wait out the first year, a full 40% of heirs withdraw their entire IRA bequest within four years. A staggering waste of opportunity.

Why does this happen? Usually because people who inherit money, even IRA money, boost their lifestyles right away. Usually, they start spending money in anticipation, before they even get their hands on a bequest.

Only the sensible and savvy learn the rules and make the money grow.

# RELYING ON YOUR LIVING TRUST AS A TAX PLAN

———

Billionaires need living trusts. Millionaires need living trusts. Middle-class folks need living trusts. Anyone who owns a house should consider a living trust.

Flip to any chapter of this book, and you will see how a living trust can do amazing things. It can protect inheritances from creditors, predators, and divorce. When you die, it can get your money to your heirs in hours or days instead of years. It can keep them out of court.

But a living trust is not a great tax planning vehicle. It's very limited when it comes to protecting your heirs from the IRS.

I can't tell you how many times clients have signed on the dotted line of a living trust document, looked up at me and said, "So, now my kids won't have to pay any taxes on this money, right? By doing this, my estate completely avoids all taxes, right?"

Wrong.

To the IRS and to your state, a living trust is "transparent." The government pretty much disregards the trust structure when it comes to figuring your taxes. Your living trust will not in and of itself prevent either estate or inheritance taxes. And income generated by trust investments does not magically become tax-free. Neither capital gains nor any other kind of tax will be avoided.

Unfortunately, because people assume that living trusts somehow help with their taxes, they may not take all kinds of other steps that could reduce or eliminate certain taxes. This may include adding features to a living trust that will help with taxes, but such features tend to benefit your heirs, not you.

Other kinds of trusts, particularly certain *irrevocable* trusts, can help a great deal with protecting your heirs from taxes. *But these are other kinds of trusts.* Living trusts are always *revocable,* hence transparent. Generally speaking, if you can change a trust and get at the money, it's your money, and it's included in your estate. Hence, your heirs may need to pay taxes on it.

## HATING ON THE DEATH TAX

The estate tax, sometimes known as the "death tax," is the tax that the federal and state governments impose on your estate at your death. Some states even impose a tax on their resident beneficiaries when they inherit, even if the deceased person was not a resident of that state (Pennsylvania). Some states count all your assets in other states, then add property located in their particular state to the top of the heap and tax the top of the heap (Oregon).

No tax seems as unfair to people as the death tax. As a result, few taxes have generated as much politics. The current estate tax has been with us since World War I, but the rates and thresholds tend to change with every administration in Washington, D.C. At this writing, they are "permanent, but subject to change at any time."

The death tax gets people downright angry. You work hard your whole life. You pay income tax on everything you earn. Whatever's left over, you save and invest. Then, when your investments earn money, you have to pay tax on the returns. If an asset goes up in value and you sell that asset, you have to pay taxes on the capital gains. But, as if all that were not enough—after all those layers of tax, if you have accumulated enough, a big chunk of your estate might go to the government.

As of this writing, the federal threshold for the estate tax is a little over $12 million per individual. In other words, if you are single and your estate has a total value above the threshold when you die, your estate has to pay 40 percent in tax to the federal government. These values are indexed to inflation, and they change every year. For a married couple, the threshold or exemption doubles, to around $24 million.

The federal estate tax comes due nine months after a death. That may seem like a lot of time, but most heirs don't realize just how quickly nine months zip by. Most heirs don't start thinking about a possible estate tax until a few months after a death, and often the assets of the deceased are not easily assessed. Investment statements may only arrive quarterly, 1099s may arrive only once a year. If the deceased failed to keep organized records, it can easily take twelve months before the heirs get an accurate accounting of absolutely everything. And many a deceased, of whatever wealth, proves not to have kept organized records at all. Family businesses and family farms must be valued and the tax paid promptly nine months after death.

In addition to the feds, some states impose their own estate taxes on anything located within their borders (see below).

## A-B TRUSTS TO AVOID ESTATE TAXES LARGELY OBSOLETE

You may have heard of an A-B trust, sometimes known as a survivor's trust or bypass trust (or exemption trust, or credit shelter trust, or family trust). You may even have one of these in an old estate plan. Prior to changes in the law in 2014, 2017 and 2019, the A-B was a common strategy used to avoid estate taxes for married couples. It solved the problem that when one spouse died, all the assets would pass into the name of the surviving spouse, often pushing the total value of the estate over the federal threshold and triggering estate taxes.

The A-B trust solved the "too big of a joint estate" problem by splitting itself on the death of one spouse, and putting the assets of the deceased into a separate bucket. The A-B trust would literally divide assets into two parts, A and B. The B part, nicknamed the "below ground" or "buried" trust, holding the assets of the deceased, would go into a "bypass trust" *controlled* by the surviving spouse. The surviving spouse could benefit from the assets, but would not technically own those assets. In an A-B trust, the survivor becomes the "A spouse," sometimes irreverently nicknamed the "alive" or "above ground" spouse.

In 2014, however, the IRS rules changed, making it unnecessary to create this artificial split between an A and B trust, at least for this purpose. As of this writing, the surviving spouse merely files a Form 706 "Portability Election" and inherits the "coupon amount," or the amount that the deceased could leave tax-free. As long as the total assets of both parties stays under two times the individual exemption (just under $11 million as of this writing), the federal estate tax will not be triggered. This, of course, assumes no "reportable" lifetime gifts were made on IRS Form 709.

There are circumstances in which an A-B trust may still be a good idea. For example, it might be needed if you are in a blended family (see Mistake #9), or if you live in a state that imposes a separate inheritance tax, what we call a "decoupled state," which we will discuss in the next section.

In general, however, the A-B living trust has become an unnecessary hassle and waste of money, creating a land mine for the future if the split fails to occur at death. You have to file a separate tax return for the B trust in addition to your personal 1040 return, and the "remainder beneficiaries," those who will inherit after the surviving spouse dies, get certain rights to information about the trust. This includes a report of what's in the trust, typically every six months or on demand. This can cause major headaches.

If you currently have an A-B trust in your estate plan, you should see an estate attorney for a review. *Now. I mean it. Put this book down and call a qualified attorney immediately.* Because, if you don't fix such a trust, and it's not appropriate for you, it's going to be a huge hassle for the surviving spouse, and the problem won't arise until one of you dies.

## DEALING WITH PARTICULAR STATES

Whether you are planning your estate, or whether you have just become an heir, you, your attorney, and your accountant need to pay a lot of attention to the estate laws of your particular state. Both the estate taxes and state tax laws vary widely.

A little history about the states versus the feds may be in order here.

Once upon a time, the estate tax exemption was only $600,000, and a lot more taxes flowed to the government when people died. The feds and the states had an agreement in which the states would get a portion of the estate tax, and both benefitted heavily.

But starting in 2001, the exemption went up to $1 million, and then kept getting higher and higher, up to the present $5 million and counting. As the exemption rose, states started complaining about getting less and less estate tax money because "not enough estates were being taxed." So, some states decided to start imposing their own, "decoupled" estate tax. We call these decoupled states because their death tax structure is not "coupled" with the federal structure.

You need to know if you live in a decoupled state, and depending on your individual circumstances, you may want to pursue alternative strategies, such as the A-B trusts discussed above, to reduce your state death tax burden.

Importantly, if your estate includes land, it matters a great deal in what state that dirt lies.

## REAL ESTATE IN YOUR STATE OR ANOTHER STATE

As we noted, decoupled states may have special estate or inheritance taxes, or both. Often, these taxes focus on "real property," meaning not just buildings, but actual land with dirt. They also focus on "tangible and intangible" personal property.

Tangible personal property is your truck, and intangible personal property is money in a bank account. *States are free to tax all of these if they are located within their state borders, regardless of the residency of the deceased.*

Indeed, some states will have a broad "estate tax" or "inheritance tax," and will impose an inheritance tax only on all forms of property located in that state. This burden falls especially hard on farmers, ranchers, and the like.

Because of this variation in laws, the location of assets must be carefully considered when preparing an estate plan.

Suppose you die with a million-dollar estate in California. But you also have a $10,000 bank account in Portland, Oregon. Guess what? Your executor is going to have to file a Portland inheritance tax return, and as of this writing, under Oregon's rules, they're going to have to include all your property in California, added to that $10,000 bank account in Oregon.

Your heirs are going to have to file an Oregon inheritance tax return and pay taxes in Oregon.

These days, many people use internet banks located in another state. If that bank is state-chartered, your money is considered to be located in that state. On the other hand, if you open a brokerage account, it's federally chartered, and not technically located in any state.

Either way, you need to understand the current laws at both the federal and state level, and do the appropriate planning. Otherwise, you could be leaving an unexpected tax trap for your heirs.

## CHARITABLE EASEMENTS

A tax strategy often used by farmers and ranchers is the

"charitable easement." It's also a somewhat complicated maneuver that does not involve a living trust. Here's how a charitable easement works, in a nutshell. When you own a piece of property, you generally own a series of additional rights related to that property. You might own the mineral rights, the water rights, and the right to improve the property and change its use. For example, if you own a piece of property, you may have the right to change it from ranch land to an industrial park.

All these additional rights have value. And therein lies a strategy for reducing taxes.

The owner of a piece of land may say, "You know what, I'm not planning to use my land's mineral rights or development rights, ever. I want to keep ranching. But I really need to reduce the value of my estate, so I don't have to pay so much property tax now, and my heirs won't have to pay estate or inheritance taxes when I die. So, I'm going to donate certain property rights to a land trust charity like the Sierra Club."

We call such a donation a "charitable easement," and it can greatly reduce the value of land for tax purposes. For example, say a piece of ranch property was worth $2 million before the charitable easement. When the rancher gives away the property's mineral and development rights to the Sierra Club, or other qualified charity, the value of the land may suddenly be reduced to $1 million—without reducing the ability of the rancher or the rancher's heirs to use and earn money from the land.

Property taxes may go down, the donor may receive a current tax benefit, and the taxable value is reduced at death.

Fortunately for the rest of us, many farmers and ranchers remain honestly disinterested in development. They focus on the great and honorable endeavor of growing food. A charitable easement can help them keep doing the work they love and we need.

## CHARITABLE TRUSTS

Charitable trusts offer another important tax strategy for a larger estate. Here's a specific example, known as a "charitable remainder unitrust."

Suppose you bought a small Picasso for $100,000, which has appreciated to $1,000,000 in value over time. If you sell your Picasso, you will have to pay a capital gains tax on the difference of $900,000. That could represent a hefty chunk of change.

Instead, talk to your attorney about setting up a charitable remainder unitrust to create what I like to call a "tax-free zone" for that $900,000. This trust will consist of assets intended for you for your life, and then what's left goes to charity. To start the process, you create the trust and you transfer your Picasso right into it.

Now, your charitable remainder unitrust can sell the Picasso *without any tax* on the transaction. Indeed, you get an income tax deduction for part of the $1 million—typically around 30 percent to 60 percent of your income. And this can be spread out into future years as well, thereby not only avoiding the tax but reducing your total taxes over the following five years.

At this point, you have a million dollars in the trust, and you have avoided taxes. The trust can then invest that money. The beneficiary of the trust can be *you* during your lifetime, your spouse during his or her lifetime, and even your kids during their lifetimes. With the unitrust, you or your heirs will receive a percentage of the growing principal of the invested trust. Each year, you simply take a snapshot of the principal, and you receive a minimum of 5 percent (or more). This income may itself be substantially tax-free for the first five years or so.

You can also make more gifts to the trust.

### CHARITY DESIGNATION LOCKED IN?

The charitable remainder unitrust has become a very popular strategy both for the philanthropic and for the charities they support.

Charities love remainder unitrusts, because when you die, or after a specified number of years, everything left in the trust goes to the charity. In return, you have not only benefitted for many years from that Picasso, but have avoided a lot of taxes on the sale of the Picasso—not just federal capital gains taxes, but often state income taxes on that money as well.

Be careful, however, which charity you choose, and look at how the designation is structured. Often, the charity will volunteer to pay all the legal fees and draft the documents, because such trusts are often structured in such a way that you cannot change the designated charity.

Federal law permits you to change the designated charity years after the trust goes into effect, but if your designee's law firm drafts the document, they are going to write the charity's name right in there.

It's another case where you need to develop a little of your own savvy, before dealing with any attorneys.

## CHARITABLE REMAINDER ANNUITY TRUST

A "charitable remainder annuity trust" is similar to a unitrust, but operates with a maximum term of twenty years. In this case, you use your assets to create a trust, which will pay you a fixed dollar amount for the life of the annuity, before a charity ultimately receives the remainder.

## CHARITABLE GIFT ANNUITY

A "charitable gift annuity" offers an even simpler structure. These annuities are operated by a number of fine nonprofits. In these arrangements, you make a significant gift to the charity, you get an income tax deduction, and then you receive a fixed income stream for the rest of your lifetime. These generally promise a rate of return much higher than a CD, often 7 percent to 8 percent, or even more. In my firm, charitable gift annuities have increased in popularity with older clients, folks in their eighties or nineties looking for a secure, hassle-free income—with a good deed attached.

## GETTING BEYOND LIVING TRUSTS

I hope you noticed that all of the above tax strategies have one thing in common: *they do not involve standard living trusts.* They all do, however, involve a tax-savvy estate planning attorney. All require an expert who will take a look at your situation and help you make serious moves in a chess game with the IRS.

Just as important is that each of the above strategies

involves a lot of advance thinking on behalf of your heirs, *thinking which must be communicated to the next generation.*

In the next chapter, Mistake #3, we'll see what happens when you wrongly assume that the people you love will know exactly what to do with your carefully built estate.

## MISTAKE

# #3

# ASSUMING YOUR TRUSTEES WILL KNOW WHAT TO DO

———

Up to now, we've focused on the importance of building living trusts, powers of attorney, and other vehicles to be used when you are gone or incapacitated.

In other words, we've focused on *creating documents.*

But in these last three mistakes, the three biggest mistakes of all, I'm going to focus on people. Why? Because not one of these beautifully written estate documents is self-executing. In the end, they do nothing but empower human beings to take certain actions. And those actions have to happen.

You may have signed your documents. But somebody else has to find your documents. Somebody else has to read them carefully, ideally with the help of an expert lawyer. Then that person must actually do what your documents say. In the right sequence. And without missing a host of deadlines. And remember, this person who serves as successor trustee *has 100 percent personal liability* for each action taken, or not taken, That's right, if the trustee messes up, a court can take away every penny that a trustee has!

Since your living trust builds the foundation of your estate plan, I will focus on choosing and enabling a trustee for your living trust. But the same advice can be followed regarding anyone you give powers of attorney, nominate as a guardian, or ask to administer any kind of document.

## TRUSTEES, EXECUTORS, AND BENEFICIARIES ALL MUST TAKE ACTION

Let me first be clear about the difference between a trustee and an executor. If you have a properly executed trust, then the person with the authority and responsibility to administer that trust is the trustee.

The person with the responsibility and authority to execute a will is the *executor.*

Ideally, the trust will be the central point where all the

appropriate assets accumulate, and where the trustee can take control of them on behalf of your beneficiaries. If you have a *living trust,* you will also have a "pour-over will" which basically moves certain types of assets into the trust when you die, if those assets are not already in the trust.

It's the responsibility of the executor of the pour-over will to make sure that the proper assets get moved into your living trust. And usually, if you have a living trust, you will designate the same person to act both as trustee and executor of the pour-over will. Both of these people should know that even in well-constructed estate plans, probate may still be required to move some assets into the living trust.

*The exceptions to the above are, however, enormous and consequential.*

## ASSETS OUTSIDE OF WILLS AND TRUSTS

As we discussed extensively in Mistake #5, IRAs, life insurance policies, annuities, and a variety of other vehicles pass by beneficiary designation on documents held by institutions, *not through trusts or wills.*

Indeed, your trustee and executor *will have no responsibility or authority* to get assets designated "Payable on Death" (POD) or "Transfer on Death" (TOD) to the proper beneficiary. Neither will your trustee or executor have any responsibility or authority to get life insurance or annuity benefits to the proper beneficiaries.

Trustees and executors may have a moral responsibility to inform beneficiaries that such assets exist, but their legal responsibility even to inform beneficiaries is often unclear, depending on local statutes.

Typically, beneficiaries are on their own when it comes to PODs, TODs, insurance policies and annuities, as such vehicles exist outside of your will and living trust. Executors and trustees may choose to help, but the institutions involved may not even speak to them.

It's the executor's job to sign all the tax returns—income tax returns and death tax returns. In order to file the death tax return, the executor needs access to all the property owned by the deceased person and this includes POD and TOD accounts, life insurance, annuities, IRAs, and 401(k)s. The executor likely will not have access to this information if other people are named beneficiaries of these accounts.

### WHAT DOES A TRUSTEE HAVE TO DO?

Let's start by focusing on the living trust, and how you can make the life of your trustee easier.

At the most general level, your trustee (or executor of your will, if you leave no living trust), must:

1. Inventory all your assets. This includes all property, all bank accounts, all investments, all household goods, everything.
2. Take control of assets by taking possession of all the proper documents at all the proper institutions. In the case of trust-owned accounts, that means getting the name of the current trustee changed on all those documents.
3. Pay the debts and expenses of the estate. These debts and expenses must be inventoried along with the assets, and a careful accounting must be kept as they are paid out. The trustee must also pay all taxes owed by the decedent and the trust.
4. Distribute assets out to the beneficiaries as specified in the trust.

This four-point to-do list may sound straightforward. But after working with thousands of estates, I am sorry to report that few trustees, no matter how smart and honest, start their job with any clue on how to do these things properly. Most have never done anything similar, and they muddle through in a fog.

Muddling in a fog may be okay, as long as your trustee is the kind of person who *will eventually* find their way through to the other side. Most will pick up the phone and call an estate attorney, usually the original attorney or firm that prepared the estate plan, and say, "Hi, my mom died, and she told us that if anything happened, we should call the lawyer. I'm looking at this trust. I guess it's in English, but it might as well be Latin for all I can understand."

At that point, we will say, "I'm so sorry to hear about your loss. Why don't you come in next Tuesday? Bring all the documents you have, along with a list of all the estate assets you know about, and we'll go over the situation. We'll tell you what needs to be done, and when."

The trustee will often arrive carrying a cardboard box full of jumbled statements and papers for us to sort through. Often, these statements and papers are of critical importance—and we have to scramble in the same way that a tax accountant must scramble when a client arrives at their office at four o'clock on the afternoon of April 15 carrying a shoebox full of receipts. Only an expert lawyer knows what to pay attention to, and what to ignore.

In addition to the financial confusion many people leave their trustees, the calls to our office come at a time of tremendous emotion and disorientation. As I said earlier when I told the story of my own mother, trustee disorientation can occur even if the deceased died quite old and had been sick for years. Much may have been left unresolved regarding everything from burial decisions to estate plans. And people are often required to face conflicts in their families which have lain dormant for years.

Siblings hated and ignored for decades may suddenly step forward. Bad memories may surface.

Of course, the death never comes at a convenient moment for the trustee (or executor, in a probate). Often, these are busy people. Indeed, a trustee may have been chosen *because* he or she was a busy professional who the parents thought they could trust.

In addition, many trustees find themselves in the "sandwich generation," stuck in their middle years taking care of their parents and their own children at the same time. Often, the trustee is the same person who has been watching tirelessly over their mother or father in assisted living or in-home care. Now the parent has died, and the trustee says, "Oh, crap, now I've got to do all this other stuff."

Entire books have been written about trust administration. Professionals dedicate careers to it. Here, we can only hit the highlights of the four primary responsibilities on the trustee's to-do list.

## 1. INVENTORY OF ASSETS

A reliable inventory of assets makes all the rest of the trustee's actions possible. But such an inventory may be elusive, and always takes longer than expected.

Properly inventorying assets, and *clarifying the ownership of those assets,* may first of all depend on the circumstances of a person's death and their state of mind at the time of their death.

In my firm, we have inventoried the assets of people who died in a house fire that burned all their records. We had other clients whose records sat in the World Trade Center on 9/11. More than once, we've had to go to court because the underlying document that determined who owned a particular account proved impossible to locate.

Your records can be lost. Your computer data can vanish. More commonly, people lose their "organizational mind" as they get older and start filing stuff in wacky places: hundred-dollar bills stuffed into books on their shelves; jars of cash buried in the backyard; gold coins plastered into walls. They may also start changing accounts around, pretty randomly, or have CDs at seventeen different institutions.

I'm sorry, but once again, if I'm not honest with you, who will be?

Sometimes inventorying basically means waiting.

If you are a trustee, you may have to wait for the mail to come in from various institutions. Sometimes you have to wait a month for a bank statement to arrive. Sometimes you have to wait three months to hear from a brokerage you didn't know about—the minimum required interval of time for them to send a statement. Sometimes you have to wait a year for a statement from other vehicles, like insurance products.

We have recommended to some clients not to finalize their inventory until January or February of the year following someone's passing. At that point, the 1099s arrive.

FINDING THE LIFE INSURANCE

According to a 2013 report on CBS News, about $1 billion in life insurance claims goes unpaid every year.

That's because even though the insurance company *knows you are dead,* they have no affirmative obligation to reach out and pay the money to your beneficiaries. The beneficiary has to submit a claim, but if the beneficiary doesn't know about the policy, that claim will never be submitted. The insurance company knows you have passed, they know who the beneficiary is, but if no one steps forward, the company holds on to the money.

I find this shocking. Obviously, insurance companies have an ethical and a moral obligation to pay out a policy, even if the law leans to their side.

## WHAT ABOUT DIGITAL ASSETS?

As of this writing, we're still living in the Wild West when it comes to finding and taking ownership of digital assets after someone dies. Some states, like California, have enacted legislation to begin to address this issue.

How many email addresses did your parents have? Facebook accounts? Twitter accounts? Dropbox storage containers? OneDrive accounts? Google Drive accounts?

When you sign up for something online, you are usually asked to accept an End User Licensing Agreement or EULA—you know, the one you have never read. When you click the "I Agree" button, you are agreeing to something on page seventeen that says, "If you die, this is who owns this electronic information, and this is who has access to it." The agreement may be contrary to what you would want, and it may be different to what you and your heirs are entitled to by law. In general, however, these agreements have held up in court.

You may really want to track down something important in your mom's email account. But what happens to that account when your mom dies will vary widely by the provider. When the provider finds out your mom has passed away, the email provider may simply shut off access to her account. And they may have rules against giving you, even as the trustee, access. Often, getting access to someone's account who has died may be in violation of the EULA.

I wish I could provide you with more specific information and an action plan around digital assets, but the situation changes every day. I can only say, "Be vigilant and do what you can in advance." If you are making your estate plan, make a list of digital assets for your heirs, with a plan for them to take control of what they need or to delete what you wish to be deleted. They may have to move quickly. If you are working with a parent, sit down with them to list everything out, and get the passwords.

## 2. TAKING CONTROL OF ASSETS

If you are a new trustee, you must establish your right to control every asset in your completed trust inventory. Even if the estate includes a living trust, that means getting your name on lots of trust asset documents where the deceased's name used to appear. This is easier said than done, and usually requires an expert attorney to get involved.

Remember Bob Sr. from Mistake #10? When he died, his name was on all his assets as an individual owner, so Bob Jr. had to go to probate court to get his name put on everything.

If Bob Sr. had created a living trust, we learned how Bob Jr. would have found that a lot easier, but he would still have had to get it done. He would have had to show up at all his father's banks and investment houses with his father's death certificate. He would have had to bring along the signed and notarized copy of the living trust and say, "Here's where it says that when Bob Sr. passes away, Bob Jr. becomes the trustee. Please give me the paperwork you need me to fill out, so that you can remove his name and put in mine as trustee controlling this account."

The same would have to be done at his father's brokerage or financial advisory accounts.

### STOCK CERTIFICATES CAN BE A BIG PROBLEM

If his father had individual stock certificates, Bob Jr. would also have to get something called the "medallion guarantee signature," which is similar to a notary, but for the Securities and Exchange Commission. If his father had thirty or forty individual share certificates, this process could become quite complex and expensive. If such a certificate became lost (or withheld by a hostile third-party like an angry sibling), Bob Jr. would have to pay a 3 percent premium to make the transfer.

If someone owns $1 million worth of stock on a single certificate, *it may cost $30,000 to replace the lost piece of paper.* I once saw that happen.

To avoid the problem of lost certificates, we recommend that our clients create something called a "street account," in which a brokerage firm holds the individual stock shares for you. It's much better to get a statement from a street account every month or quarter than to try to hold onto such valuable pieces of paper. You may also have the transfer agent hold onto the shares, but in my experience, they are less convenient than a street account.

What's the overall message to Bob Sr., and everyone creating their estate plan? Make sure that your living trust is properly "funded," with all relevant assets properly transferred into it. Maintain good records. And for heaven's sake, make sure your trustee can find your records.

## PODS, TODS, AND OTHER ASSETS OUTSIDE OF TRUSTS AND WILLS

Accounts which have a "Payable on Death" (POD) or "Transfer on Death" (TOD) designation often become a major pain for trust administrators and beneficiaries. As discussed earlier (see Mistake #10) such assets move outside of the living trust and the will—and are not technically the responsibility of your trustee to find and distribute.

In theory, if you have four children, and you properly list all four on a POD, each one can just show up at the institution and demand a quarter of the asset (or benefit, or distribution, etc.), when you die.

In practice, it's often not so simple, and whenever possible, you should try to minimize assets with a POD or TOD designation.

Why? When your assets are included in your living trust, all the information is updated at once, and control of the assets remains clear. You can also use language like "distribute all these funds equally among my surviving children and the estates of my deceased children."

But when you had set up that annuity with a POD years ago, you probably signed it and forgot all about it. Suppose you had only two kids when you first set it up, and now you have four, but you never updated the document? Suppose you listed all four, but one of your children has now passed away?

The result will be a mess.

Or, suppose back when your son, Johnny, started his business, you set up a joint bank account with him, into which you placed $100,000. What happens to that account when you die? You may have said to Johnny, "I'm giving you $100,000 to start your business, but remember that when I die, you need to put that money back into the pot to be shared with your siblings." When you actually die, however, Johnny will talk to his lawyer and his lawyer will tell him that he can keep the whole $100,000. It belongs solely to him. And the lawyer may be right.

The same will be true of that annuity on which you only got around to listing your two older children. They will be under no obligation to share that money with their siblings.

As you can see, the unanticipated consequences of multiple designations and accounts can escalate quickly. Along with hurt feelings and unfair benefits distributed among your loved ones. Your goal and the goal of your estate planner must be to anticipate all consequences.

### 3. PAYING DEBTS AND EXPENSES

Whether an estate passes to the next generation smoothly via a living trust, or whether it triggers the hassle of probate, the biggest issues may revolve around debts and creditors.

The main reason probate takes so long and requires so many crazy actions like publishing notices in the paper (see

Mistake #10: Letting Your Family Go to Probate), is that probate exists so that creditors can get paid. They have a powerful lobby in state legislatures.

Banks, lien holders, mortgage holders, and investment companies holding outstanding debt are the folks who complicate probate. They want to know who died, and they want to collect what they think they are owed by the deceased.

Indeed, as an heir, you can think of probate as a lawsuit you file against yourself to protect your creditors. You even have to tell them to come after you, by sending *them* notices.

The same requirement to satisfy creditors applies to the trustee of a living trust. The financial obligations are almost identical to those of an heir or executor going through probate. In trust administration, you also have to find out who the creditors are, and you have to pay them. But there's no requirement for formal notification to creditors, and everything can happen outside of court.

If you don't pay up, the creditors may be able to come after the trustee, personally. The way most revocable living trusts are written—and under most state law—the assets are available to pay the debts of the person who passed away. *Irrevocable trusts* can create substantial protection for certain assets (see Mistake #6: Letting Third Parties Take Advantage of Your Beneficiaries).

I don't think these laws will change. Creditors would block the use of trusts if they couldn't go into a revocable trust and collect money they were owed.

The federal government, state governments, and state agencies are considered super creditors with much increased rights over other kinds of creditors. For example, a trustee may be required to notify a state agency about paying restitution for a deceased person who was previously incarcerated. If the deceased was on Medicaid or a state healthcare benefit program, the trust may have to pay back what the person received.

## COSTS OF THE LAST ILLNESS

One of the biggest costs often facing an estate are the unpaid bills from doctors and nursing facilities following a long, final illness. These may be staggering, as a nursing home alone can run from $5,000 to $30,000 a month.

As with other debt and creditor situations, we suggest using a law firm with an ability to prepare your accounting documents, or work with a qualified accountant. This helps to finalize debt reconciliation with doctors, nursing homes, and the like.

There are often attendant legal issues, and you will want bulletproof recordkeeping on all your actions.

## WHAT ABOUT CREDIT CARDS?

Does an estate have to pay off credit card debt? Well, yes.

However, if there's no probate hearing in which the credit card company has been notified, and if the balance lies under say $10,000, in my experience, the credit card company often chooses not to pursue the matter. They may simply not find it worth their time and cost to go after the estate. Deciding if this is the right thing to do rests with the trustee and executor. My job here is to tell you what happens in the real world, and to leave it to you to decide what's best for you.

## FUNERAL COSTS ARE OFTEN CONTENTIOUS

Let me end the debts discussion by pointing out that the first cost to an estate, and the most immediate, will be the funeral. It can also be the most contentious. Most cemeteries and funeral homes don't send bills. They demand upfront payment. And oftentimes, the people with the least money want the biggest, most expensive funerals—don't ask me why.

Often, a child or other relative will have to step up to pay for a funeral, expecting to be reimbursed from the estate later. Not surprisingly, this can lead to conflict. Who bought all those flowers? Did he have to have the pewter casket?

As noted earlier, you can save your loved ones a lot of money and conflict by giving them the gift of pre-need planning. Under these arrangements, you go down to a funeral home and pick out everything you like: casket, flowers, the works. You write a check, say for $10,000, not to the funeral home or cemetery, but to an insurance company. If the funeral home goes bankrupt or burns down, you still have your money with the insurance company. When you die, a claim will be made by your relatives or friends, and they will complete the funeral according to your wishes, right down to the six dozen carnations and the Studebaker-themed casket with the steering wheel option you specified.

Pre-need planning need not be awkward. Think of it as removing sixty or seventy of the nine thousand things your loved ones are going to have to do when you die. Think of it as making their job easier.

## 4. DISTRIBUTING THE ASSETS

On the face of it, nothing should be easier than distributing assets to the beneficiaries of a will or a trust. In practice, it does not happen immediately after death, and can get pretty complicated. Indeed, nothing may require more help from an attorney.

Suppose a will says, "I leave everything to my son, and if

my son passes away, then I leave everything to his children."
Sounds pretty straightforward, right?

Okay, but if the son has indeed passed away and we want
to leave everything to the son's children, what constitutes a
parent-child relationship? A parent-child relationship may
be defined differently in every state. Sometimes people who
aren't blood relatives are considered children, sometimes not.

Often, the problem arises from wills and trusts which are
written too simply.

*There, I've said it.* Plenty of people distrust lawyers and want
short forms, even "one-pagers," which do not create nearly
enough specificity down the line.

Guess what? Even eight-pagers don't work.

Suppose a "simple" will or trust says, "When I die, distribute my estate to my children." What does that mean? If you
have three kids, and they're all alive, no problem. Each gets
a third. But, what if one child has died? Who gets that child's
share? The will or trust does not say, "Distribute only to my
living children," and it does not say outright that if one of
the children has died, their third goes to their estate. The
"simple" has just become needlessly complex.

How will a judge rule if this issue goes to court? I cannot tell you. Courts don't just follow statutes that a state legislature passes; they go by "case law." Courts want to know how previous judges ruled in these kinds of cases. Case law fills law books, and you will find thousands of law books in a law library. How do you know the opposing attorney won't find the one case out there which will contradict your client's desires? And how much money will everyone spend finding out?

## WHEN THINGS GO WRONG

With even the best-written trusts, trustees can get confused. They can make the wrong moves. And sometimes, they do nothing at all.

Here's a common problem. A man will call me and say, "Mr. Cunningham, my mother died two years ago, and my brother was supposed to divide up the assets among the children. We buried Mom, but then we didn't hear anything from my brother. I think he's the trustee, but he hasn't given us a copy of anything. A while back, he stopped returning my phone calls, and when I go over to Mom's old house, I can see he's still living there, but he won't open the door. He just yells at me to go away. What do I do?"

What happened? The trustee has broken trust with his brother. He thought to himself, "Hey, if I sell this house, I'm going to be out of a home. It's nice here. If I just do nothing, maybe my brother will go away."

A trustee cannot use the house for his benefit alone, if the house was given to benefit all the children. The trustee's brother and the other beneficiaries may have to hire us to sue his brother. In court, we will ask to have the trustee removed and replaced. Or, more commonly, the trustee will give in, sell the house, and get a move on before the case goes that far. Either way, it will get ugly and cost everyone a lot of time and money. There will be no more Thanksgivings where the whole, extended family comes together.

In this case, the parents not only chose the wrong trustee, they failed to put in place a trust protector (see below) who could have resolved the issue quickly and easily.

## THE STALE TRUST

Often, a living trust is set up with the assumption that certain actions will take place immediately upon the death of one of the parties. It may be an A-B trust (see Mistake #4), which must be split into two trusts at the death of the B party—but the trustee never took the trouble to execute the split. Maybe the trustee never even realized the split had to occur. Ten years later, when the second spouse dies, the trust simply no longer makes sense, with dire tax consequences.

Here's another example of a stale trust:

Mom dies, and her trust is set up assuming her house will be sold and the proceeds divided up among a set of heirs.

But the sale never takes place—once again, the oldest brother, named as trustee, just moves in and lives there. But this time, maybe the other siblings are fine with that arrangement, because the economy is down and everyone wants to wait.

Five, six, ten years go by before the house gets sold.

Unfortunately, the estate must now pay the embedded capital gains on the sale of the house, starting on the day Mom died. A valuation expert will have to figure out what the house was valued at ten years earlier at the time of death. And all of a sudden, the kids may be underwater on their trust, owing taxes instead of benefitting from the estate.

## MISTAKES MAY INCLUDE GUNS

I can't help but mention here that a lot of people make mistakes involving the deceased's firearms. I'm serious. This is a major problem in the estate world.

People may walk into the home of their deceased parent, find a firearm, and say, "I'll just take that home for safekeeping." Or, the heirs will gather in the house to identify the stuff they want for themselves, and someone will just begin passing out the guns from dad's collection.

For starters, the gun laws are different all across the country. Certain firearms are legal in certain states and prohibited in other states. Trustees will throw these guns in the trunks of their cars and drive across the state line to deliver a firearm to a beneficiary, committing an inadvertent federal felony just by crossing into another state.

Then, in their home state, which may require specific safety certificates and registrations, the heir now owns a firearm without any of the proper registrations or paperwork. Indeed, the heir may be personally prohibited from owning a firearm, because the heir may be under a restraining order, be a convicted felon, or fall under a host of other categories. As of this writing, for example, people in California, Oregon, Washington, Alaska, Montana, Idaho, Nevada, Arizona, Hawaii and Guam who possess a medical marijuana card cannot legally possess a firearm.

Just as commonly, when a gun collector dies (usually a man), his wife may want to get rid of his stockpile of firearms. She scoops them up, tosses them into her car, and drives down to a gun dealer to sell them off. If you talk to any gun dealer, you will hear the same stories. "A couple of times a month," one dealer told me, "a little old lady will come in. She'll drive into the parking lot, take us out to her car, pop the trunk, and show us a pile of pistols, rifles, scopes, and huge boxes of ammo."

Her attempt to sell these weapons in this manner actually constitutes a felony. It's also dangerous.

I don't want to dwell on the hot-button issue of guns and ammo—but they are an example of the kinds of errors that can be made very quickly by unthinking heirs and trustees.

Guns are also an example of why you need to pick the right person as a trustee. In fact, you may want to choose a special trustee just for guns and ammo. Your trustee should not hesitate to get professional advice.

## CHOOSING A TRUSTEE

How do most people choose a trustee? What process will they follow to pick a candidate for a job which involves the proper handling of attorneys, bank officers, gun collections, and possibly millions of dollars?

Usually, mom and dad sit around the kitchen table filling out estate documents. They come to the blank for filling in the trustee's name. Who will they choose to execute their will and trust when they fall ill or pass away?

"Well, I don't know," says Dad. "Of the three kids, Johnny's the oldest. We'll pick him as trustee. It should be the oldest, right? As an honor?"

Then the documents are filed away in a drawer for thirty years, and pulled out only when both mom and dad have died.

Well, Johnny was a great guy at twenty-one, but will he be the right person to manage an estate as trustee at fifty-one? Does he have the time, the drive, and the integrity to do this right?

Thirty years later, maybe Johnny himself isn't so sure. Maybe Johnny has grown into a super-busy businessman with little time or interest in his parent's trust.

Or, maybe Johnny hates paperwork and lives on a fishing boat in Tampa Bay, without a phone.

## THREE'S A CROWD

Then again, back at that kitchen table thirty years earlier, maybe mom and dad just couldn't decide. Maybe they didn't want to make any of their kids angry, so Mom said, "I know, let's name all three of the kids as joint trustees!"

Now, all these years later, when the three kids are middle-aged, they have a serious problem. Now they see each other as three cooks in the same, ugly kitchen.

Johnny and Eddie never agree, so Lisa usually has the veto, and she usually goes with Eddie. Anger frequently flares, and it's not really the kids' fault. Anytime you have more than one trustee, it's tough to make any big decision. Even tough to see the decision through.

Should Johnny, Eddie, and Lisa sell the family land in Hawaii to a developer? With only one trustee, a decision can be fast. But with three, things can get complicated and stay complicated.

Say that Eddie and Lisa agree to sell. As a majority, they sign the papers, and the process of the sale begins. But Johnny hates the idea of cutting down all those coconut trees, and refuses to sign. The company buying the land gets nervous. Sure, they've won a majority vote among the trustees, but what if that one rogue trustee goes off and does something to block the sale down the line? The buyers may think, "Unless all three trustees sign off, we'd better look elsewhere."

A good attorney would have advised mom and dad to choose a single trustee—sometimes two if they get along. And an attorney would have advised them to update their estate plan as their kids grew and their circumstances changed. That one, cozy, kitchen table session just wasn't enough.

## GO WITH EXPERIENCE?

When people sit down to choose a trustee, they must sometimes choose between a family member with no experience and a family member who has administered a trust before. Both situations may present an issue.

Someone who has never administered a trust may be starting blind. But someone who has done it before may be burned out. Here's a common situation:

Mom and dad sit down at the kitchen table to fill out their trust documents, and Mom says, "Well, my sister was the trustee for my mother, and she was the trustee for both my brothers' estates. She's done this three or four times, so she's an expert by now. I want to name her."

Well, she'd better check with her sister, because her sister may not want the job. I have plenty of clients who come in and say, "Darn it (or a much stronger expletive), this is the *fifth trust* I'm going to have to administer, and everyone keeps naming me, because I'm the person in the family who apparently does all of this. Well, sorry, I don't want to do trust administration anymore. It's a pain in the ass.

I don't want to spend the final years of my life handling everyone else's estates. I'd rather garden. Or head off on a cruise. Or just about anything else. How can I get out of this?"

## MORE FACTORS TO CONSIDER

Regardless of experience, do not name someone as trustee "to honor" them. Name someone who you believe to be trustworthy and responsible.

Let's start with that word "responsible." Merely "well-intentioned" will not cut it. You want someone who can get the job done.

If you don't have a friend or family member you consider responsible, what I call a "civilian," you may want to consider a "private professional fiduciary." These are people who hold themselves out to the world as professional trust administrators. Some states actually have a registry for private professional fiduciaries and may require them to act under a bond (see below for more on bonds). Some states don't regulate the profession at all. A trustee has tremendous and independent power, so if you go the professional route, do your due diligence.

Whether you choose a civilian or professional trustee, consider everyone's age carefully.

If you are in your fifties or sixties, and you name a trustee about your same age, remember that that person *will age right along with you.* It's likely that you will have reached your eighties or nineties by the time you need your trustee. A trustee who's also eighty or ninety years old may be in worse shape than you. Or already gone.

Professional fiduciaries are often second-career folks who start in their fifties, so they may not be around when the time comes. You may be dealing with their successor, or they may have named no successor at all. As part of choosing a private professional, you must ask, "What is your succession plan? Who's the next person in line? What happens if you are hit by a bus?"

If you choose any individual, you must review your choice periodically. People change. Their circumstances change. They pass away. See Mistake #2: Forgetting to Keep Up with Changes and Staying in Touch.

## CONSIDER A TRUST COMPANY

If you can't find the right individual family member or friend to take on the job of trustee, and you don't like the idea of an independent professional fiduciary, you might want to consider a "trust company" to administer your living trust.

Trust companies are institutions or branches of institutions that provide trust administration as a business. They will typically name a person to administer your trust, but that person will change over time, just as your bank representative may change over time. You are naming the *trust company* (usually a bank), *not* their representative, as your trustee.

## TRUST COMPANY VS. TRUST BANK: KNOW THE DIFFERENCE

Trust Companies and Trust Banks are not the same, not even close—and they charge radically different fees.

A "traditional" trust bank operates as a division of a large, traditional, general-purpose bank. The traditional trust bank handles both trust administration *and investment* of the trust funds. Traditional trust banks charge the highest fees, and they've been increasing their minimums over the years. Typically, you will have to pay them 1 percent to 2 percent of the total estate value each year. Over time, that can really add up.

Traditional trust banks also often invest in *proprietary funds,* so the bank earns revenue not only when they serve as trustee, but when the bank, as trustee, buys investments from the same bank that created the investments. Getting paid five times on the same money isn't a bad deal for the large banks, but may be a bad deal for you and your beneficiaries.

The alternative is a more modern approach which is a "trust company." These are smaller institutions, with the important difference that they *don't handle the investments* within the estate. These non-traditional trust banks perform only a fiduciary function, and leave the investing to a third-party financial advisor, typically of your choice. When you walk in, a non-traditional trust bank looks less like a bank and more like an accountant's office. Fees at non-traditional trust banks generally tend to run 50 percent to 80 percent lower than at a traditional trust bank.

## LOCATION MATTERS

The location of the bank and the assets matter. A lot.

If you live in a high-tax jurisdiction, you should consider a trust bank which operates only in a state without state income tax, because this may help your trust avoid your own state taxes. If you live in a state without state income taxes, this may not be an issue.

The state residency of the beneficiaries and the trustees will also matter.

Hence, a California resident may choose a trust bank in Nevada, South Dakota, Tennessee, or Alaska; so that after their death, continuing trusts for their loved ones don't pay state income tax.

However, if you are a Nevada resident and you name a California resident as the trustee of your trust, and this person actually starts serving as trustee, your Nevada-based trust will become subject to California state income taxation.

Astounding? Yes. Do you need a tax-savvy estate attorney to consult on these complex choices? Without question.


## LET'S TALK ABOUT HONESTY

The chief advantage of naming a trust company or trust bank is simple. It won't steal from your trust. I consider this a big plus. Why? Because the chief disadvantage of naming any *individual*, civilian or professional, as your trustee is equally simple. He or she can easily steal from your trust. Why? Because no one is watching what they do.

Throughout this book, I have urged you to create a living trust in order to avoid probate court. But yes, in a court proceeding, other people *are at least watching.* Indeed, with a court-supervised proceeding, any executor who is named for an estate must typically operate with a bond.

A bond is not exactly a form of insurance, but if the executor steals the money in your estate, the bonding company will replace the money. If the bond is for $100,000 and the executor steals $100,000, the bonding company will deposit $100,000 back into the estate. After that, of course, the bonding company will go after the thief to get the money back.

Trusts do not typically operate with bonds. And yes, thefts by the executors of wills and the trustees of living trusts do occur.

Some years ago, I was handling a probate case for a modest estate. The deceased left no will or living trust, but an executor had been named by the court. That executor was my client. About a month before the final hearing, my firm filed an accounting with the court in which we said, "Your honor, here's all the money we started with. Here's all the money that went out. Here's what's left, and we are pleased to say that all the numbers add up."

A couple of days before the hearing, the judge asked, in a tentative ruling, "I want to know exactly how much cash this estate now has on hand. I know you filed this petition a month or two ago, so how much does the executor have today?"

He had asked a reasonable question, and I called my client. She picked up the phone and said, flat out, "Well, Jim, I gambled all the money away."

Now I have a dilemma, because my client has told me she

has committed a crime. She has admitted to embezzling the money from the estate, but because of attorney-client privilege, I cannot tell the judge. On the day of the hearing, however, I have to stand in front of his bench.

"Okay, Mr. Cunningham," says the judge, "tell me, how much is now in this estate?"

"Your honor," I reply, "there's nothing in the estate. The estate has zero dollars."

"Well, what happened to all the money?"

"I can't tell you."

Now the judge gets a little angry. "The heck you can't tell me. What happened to that money? You are the lawyer for the estate. You must know what happened."

I say, "Your honor, I can't tell you what happened to the money. That's privileged."

You can see the light go on in his head. His eyebrows go up. "Ah," he nods. "Okay, I get it."

Right then and there, the judge signed a bench warrant for my client's arrest. She was picked up the following weekend and charged with embezzlement.

In the story about the gambling executor, it turned out that she stole the money and blew it in less than a week. If a trustee decides to steal from a trust, actually holding her accountable for her crime can take a year or longer with a trust as opposed to a will, and drain tens of thousands of dollars in a way that no one notices. No lawyers or judges will be around to see it happening.

The power and independence of trustees provide the key benefit to living trusts, but that same power and independence means you must choose your trustees very wisely, indeed. If you have the slightest doubt about a potential trustee, choose someone else.

You should also consider the use of a trust protector.

## THE ROLE OF THE TRUST PROTECTOR FOR A CONTINUING TRUST

A trust protector is typically an attorney or other professional who has the power to make limited changes to a trust without going to court. He or she can also replace a trustee if the trust protector thinks it's necessary. We discussed the importance of these folks earlier, especially in regard to minors and disabled beneficiaries (see Mistakes #7 and #10), and in the case of an IRA Stretch Trust (see Mistake #5).

Is the trust protector watching the operation of the trust at all times? No. The trust protector typically looks in on the trust and intervenes only when someone makes a complaint. One of the trust beneficiaries or an interested third-party will say, "I'm concerned about the way this trustee is doing his job," or "Wouldn't it be better if the trust said this?"

Not every trust requires a trust protector, but I generally recommend one for any "continuing trust," which does more than simply distribute assets on your death.

A continuing trust is any trust which continues on for a year or more after your death, or, it operates when you are incapacitated. It says, "When I die, hold this money aside for my disabled child," or, "Hold this money aside for my child until they reach a certain age," or, "Hold this money to pay for my continuing care."

PREVENTING SCAMS

As people age, they are often unable to look out for themselves. They become unable to handle their own affairs and look to others for guidance. At age eighty or ninety, friends start dying, trusted professionals retire, and a spouse may already be gone.

Their world shrinks. And as a result, *they become vulnerable to false friendships.*

Here's one common scam. People in prison are often told, "Hey, when you get out, you should go on Craigslist and answer an ad for a home health worker. People looking for home health workers pay under the table, and they don't usually bother to do background checks."

Such people may begin working in an older person's home and quickly become the elder's new "best friend." After a while, this felon gets the shut-in to resign as trustee of their estate, or switches out the trustee and appoints the felon as trustee—long before the shut-in dies. Our firm has received calls from police departments telling us that our clients had fallen victim to this kind of elder abuse, and we needed to get involved.

A trust protector can remove this new trustee right away with a single signature on a piece of paper—and stop the bleeding until the family figures out what's happening. Without a trust protector, family members will have to go to court and use their own money to protect mom.

Let me repeat, however, that a trust protector is not actively monitoring the situation of the trust. Someone else must see what's happening and call in the trust protector when needed.

You can see why it generally makes sense to name a trust protector with the deep expertise needed to spot issues and make the right changes. Often, you will choose to name the attorney who prepares your estate plan as the trust protector (with successors in his or her firm). But, as I noted in earlier chapters, you can provide the name of anyone to take on this important role.

Just be sure they know what they are doing.

## FIRST, DO NO HARM

Our firm offers a guidebook to our clients who become trustees of estates. It runs about one hundred pages, single-spaced. Like the book you hold in your hands, our little guidebook is no substitute for legal advice. But it helps. We tell trustees, "Don't tick off your siblings. At least, not unnecessarily."

And indeed, the first thing many trustees do is tick somebody off. Then, that somebody goes to a lawyer. Then things get ugly.

First and foremost, trustees must be level-headed people who can handle the emotionally charged time after the death of a loved one. That's why bringing in the pros may be best.

Even if the estate names an individual as trustee, rather than a trust company or independent professional, that trustee may choose—and I recommend—to use an expert lawyer for trust administration.

Certainly, as I noted above, the estate's original law firm will often play a key role in guiding the first steps of the trustee. Indeed, law firms will often write their contact information directly into a trust, with instructions for the trustee to contact them immediately. The firm puts its phone number right into the document, and there's nothing wrong with that. No one knows the trust better than the people who wrote it.

But, when it comes to choosing a law firm to do long-term trust administration, the trustee must exercise caution and do some due diligence. (See also the Introduction, on choosing an estate planning firm in the first place.)

Many lawyers know how to set up an estate plan, *but they do not necessarily have enough experience to know how to effectively administer an estate plan after a death.* In fact, this kind of work often requires an entirely different personality type and skillset. Trust administration lawyers must be extremely diligent and detail oriented over a longer period of time than a lawyer who is creating an estate plan. They cannot object to repetition and routine.

Lawyers, on the other hand, are often interested in the initial puzzle, in reading situations with their "legal brains" and fighting lively battles. "Thinking like a lawyer" may be important at one stage in the game, but a detriment in another.

Boeing designs aircraft, Southwest flies them. There's a reason that Boeing does not fly their own aircraft, and a reason that Southwest does not build their own planes. The skillsets are very distinct.

A larger law firm will have attorneys dedicated to estate planning. Then they will have separate staff and attorneys dedicated to trust administration. A kind of artificial wall will separate these two functions, because these functions work best when the right people are focused on the right job.

Then again, the very best trust administration lawyer will be helpless if the trust has become obsolete by the time it has to be administered. In Mistake #2, we'll see just how easily that can happen.

# FORGETTING TO KEEP UP WITH CHANGES AND NOT STAYING IN TOUCH

———

Of the many misconceptions about estate planning, none is worse than the widespread notion that you need to do it just once, sometime in your fifties.

People think they can wait until they turn fifty-five, sign some documents, fund their trusts, and then stick the papers in a drawer and forget about the whole subject for the next thirty years. Maybe, just maybe, they'll remember to tell the kids about the drawer before they die.

Problem is, the world will change during those thirty years. So will your accounts, your relationships, your kids' relationships, and your online passwords.

But the papers you stuck in the drawer won't change. Not by themselves, anyway.

And yes, some people do die before fifty-five.

## LET'S START WITH THE CHANGES

There are two kinds of changes that can render your estate plan useless—or worse than useless—over the course of the years.

The first are changes in the law. These come faster than you imagine, *because the law changes every single day.*

I am not kidding. Literally every single day a new case gets published, and because the law operates not just by statute but by *case law,* that means judges statewide or nationwide will be influenced by the new cases to make different decisions than those anticipated by your original plan. And of course, the statutes themselves change. The U.S. Congress, your state legislature, *or the legislatures where your beneficiaries reside* will pass a new tax law. At first, this law may seem to have nothing to do with your estate—until a lawyer examines the tax implications for your trust structure.

These changes in law may have major implications even in smaller estates. But I must repeat that often the smaller estates matter the most to people. Why? Because people with fewer means may be far more dependent on the results of an inheritance. If $100,000 has to be split up sixteen ways, it may really matter to those sixteen people.

Spending $10,000 of that precious money to resolve the legal issues created by an out-of-date trust may create a family catastrophe.

## CHANGES IN *EVERYONE'S* LIVES

The second kind of changes occur in your own life and the lives of your loved ones. These changes also arrive a whole lot faster than you ever imagined.

Anytime your family experiences a birth, a death, a marriage, or a divorce, your estate plan needs to be pulled out of that drawer to see if it still works the way you want it to work, considering the life change. You should reevaluate your documents anytime you or a beneficiary moves to another state, every time you buy a house, sell a house, invest in property, or change your brokerage investment accounts.

Do new assets have to get moved into your trust? Do the names of beneficiaries, trustees, and guardians need revision? And what about your online accounts?

## ACCESSING ACCOUNTS

Throughout this book, we have discussed the enormous issues beneficiaries often face in accessing the accounts they have inherited. Are the beneficiaries named as trustees? Do they even *know* about their beneficiary designation on an IRA or an insurance policy? Have you updated those designations properly, on all the right documents?

As the world goes more and more digital, however, you also need to think seriously about passing on account access information like passwords to your digital assets—everything from your email, to your Facebook pages, to your bank accounts.

At some point, physical bank branches may disappear altogether.

Whatever you decide to pass on digitally will need to be updated—and frequently.

## THE LIFE CYCLE OF PLANNING

I find it helpful to map the constant changes needed in personal estate planning to some of the major life events in life.

### AT AGE EIGHTEEN

As we discussed, every eighteen-year-old needs to sign

a durable power of attorney for property and an advance healthcare directive (durable power of attorney for healthcare), along with a HIPAA authorization (see Introduction and Mistake #8).

Hardly anyone realizes the importance of these documents—until something happens and they don't exist. When your kids turn eighteen, you become legally helpless to take care of them when they may need you most. Without these papers, you no longer have access to their healthcare information or the right to make vital health decisions for them if they get hit by a car. You can no longer fix problems with their bank accounts.

You can't even check their grades at college.

Eighteen-year-olds are not immortal. Mental health issues often arise in college. And if your child becomes incapacitated, someone will have to even deal with that battered, old car you put in their name.

No papers? You may end up petitioning a court just to help your own kid.

## ACQUIRING ASSETS

During your twenties and beyond, you will begin acquiring assets—small or large. That means you need to add at least a valid will to your set of estate documents. Even if you have only a tiny bank account, a car, and a big screen TV, you should care who would get that stuff if you fall off a cliff while rock climbing.

If you buy a house or other property, you may also need to create a living trust, or you may be creating a major headache for your family if you die.

Even when you're only twenty-five, if you buy property, life gets serious. Mistake #10 applies big time. Please don't send your family to probate court.

## HAVING CHILDREN

With children come innumerable responsibilities. One is estate planning. If you have not done so already, you must visit with a lawyer to discuss creating an estate plan to protect them if you die or become incapacitated.

Even more importantly, you must nominate a guardian for your children if something happens to you and your spouse. Choosing guardians for persons and for property is not easy and should never been done casually. Take a look at Mistake #10 for some advice.

## MORE CHILDREN, MORE ASSETS

Over the years, you cannot neglect the changes needed to your plan as more children arrive. And you must pull your estate plan out of the drawer for review as possible guardians become unavailable or no longer trusted.

I know of a boy who was in grade school when his mother died. Then his father died when he was a sophomore in high school. It happens.

The parents had named a guardian who had lived near their house in California, but later moved to Connecticut. The child said to the judge, "You know what? I don't want to move to Connecticut. I want to stay here with my friends." The judge agreed, and the court named a different guardian. Was the new guardian a person the parents would have chosen if they had kept their plan up to date? We'll never know.

For the sake of your kids, you must also make serious estate plan revisions if you divorce or experience a major financial change.

Have you become a little wealthy? Congratulations. You owe it to yourself, your family, and your community to investigate the various ways you can protect your assets against predators and taxes. You should investigate charitable trusts and other vehicles to both help your community and guard your estate.

## AGE FIFTY-FIVE

A significant series of changes to your plan need to start when you hit middle age. If you never made a plan, this is *really the time to get it done.*

But when you arrive at age fifty-five or so, you will also find that your parents are aging rapidly, and you need to make sure they have *their estate plan* in order. If none exists, help them create it. If one already exists, get it reviewed by an attorney.

By now, you may have joined the "sandwich generation," taking care of both your children and your parents at the same time. Your estate plan must now deal with the impact your own death or incapacity would have on *both* generations. The parent becomes the child, and the child becomes the parent.

## AGE SIXTY

At age sixty, you will start thinking more seriously about retirement. As of this writing, you can potentially start taking out social security at age sixty-three, though you will get less return than if you wait. A financial advisor can help you make crucial decisions, such as when to start taking social security. But as you head toward retirement, you also need to review your estate plan carefully, especially the way it handles retirement vehicles like your IRA and 401(k). Reread Mistake #5.

## AGE SIXTY-FIVE

At sixty-five, more changes will likely come in your life.

For starters, you will be auto-enrolled into Medicare, which proves a lifesaver to many. A lot of people now work until age sixty-five, when they get "RIF'd." That is, they become part of a Reduction in Force. Without Medicare, they would be paying two or three grand a month on health insurance.

No longer working? Using Medicare and perhaps another public benefit program? Get someone to review your estate plan and make sure you don't lose those benefits or let the state take your house when you die to pay the state back.

## AGE SEVENTY

At age seventy, you need to begin thinking about taking your minimum distributions from your retirement accounts, which must happen at seventy-two. We discussed the significant estate issues related to IRA distributions in Mistake #5. Fail to take these distributions or understand how they impact your estate plan, and you may be creating huge problems for yourself and your heirs.

Please believe me that even if you read Mistake #5 carefully, you *still* "don't know what you don't know" about retirement accounts. For example, a seventy-year-old may be able to transfer a 401(k) to a younger spouse using a court order and delay minimum distributions to take advantage of a longer tax deferment on the account.

Few people know about such maneuvers except savvy financial planners and estate attorneys. That's why you need to seek an expert for a review.

### AGE SEVENTY-FIVE

After seventy, things often start going wrong with people's health. *It's also the age when the people you named as potential trustees and guardians may be getting too old.* At the same time, the professionals who have been assisting you with legal and financial issues may be retiring from their work.

Does your plan need updating for these changes? Almost certainly, the answer is yes.

By seventy-five, everyone also faces the strong possibility that a major physical or cognitive issue will arise for at least one of two spouses. Such events definitely require a review of estate plans. Are guardianship mechanisms adequate? Are spouses protected?

Meanwhile, what's happening in the lives of your heirs? At this point, they will be hitting middle age, and will have far more complex financial lives to consider.

Do you need to think about the way your trust transfers assets to a wealthy child, or to prevent a big tax hit? See Mistake #7 and Mistake #4.

### EIGHTY AND UP

At eighty, it's now very likely that a spouse will develop a significant impairment—not necessarily severe, but something of concern. At this point, if your trust structure is not in order, and if you have not planned around protecting your public benefits, you and your estate become very vulnerable financially.

Without some planning, a stroke followed by nursing home bills of $10,000 a month can wipe you out. See Mistake #8: Forgetting to Plan for Disability.

### HOW DO ESTATE PLANS FAIL?

Some estate plans fail not because they were badly written from the start.

Others fail because no one updated them as the years went by. No one stayed in touch with the people named in the plan to see what was happening in their lives. No one stayed in touch with the planning and financial professionals needed to keep things on track.

Say you decide to refinance your house. To do that, the bank says you must pull the property out of your living trust temporarily. Fine and dandy. But then you have to take the trouble to put it back into your trust. Forgot to do that? Now you are sending your heirs into probate.

When your kids were born, your brother was a healthy and well-adjusted forty-year-old, and you nominated him as guardian if anything happened to you. Now, your kids are teenagers, and your brother is a divorced, sick, broke, drunk, cranky, unemployed fifty-one-year-old. You hardly talk, and he's no proper role model for your children. There's no way you'd want him watching over them and your finances now. But, if you get hit by a car before you change the name on those papers, it's too late. Boom, your kids are reporting to your wayward brother.

You're married and had an A-B trust created in 2012, before the law changed in 2014, 2017, and 2019 (see Mistake #4). Now the whole plan doesn't make any sense. Did you pay attention to that email from your attorney in 2014, 2017, and 2019 telling you to contact him for a review? Ignore the question and your spouse and your kids may face a tax mess when you die twenty years from now. Or, the whole plan may be tossed aside and your heirs will be headed for probate when you die, because it has become "stale." In fact, that stale plan may be worse than no plan at all, because it twists things in a way that no one, even a court, can quite untangle.

Back before you married, you named your best friend as your beneficiary on your $1 million IRA, with no successor beneficiary if anything happened to him. Ten years later, you're married, and your friend has died of cancer. Unfortunately, his name is still written into that IRA document, filed away somewhere at your bank. I had a case just like this. The heirs ended up with $50,000 in probate fees and the $1 million IRA was diminished by $450,000 in income tax. No kidding.

## NOT TRANSACTIONAL, BUT RELATIONAL

If you are a person with children, a house, and any means, you need to think about your estate plan not as a document but as a relationship. Not just with your family and your heirs, but with your attorney and your financial advisors.

Transactions may be one-off affairs. But relationships need ongoing contact. They need maintenance. They need care and feeding.

You should be meeting with your financial advisor at least once a year, preferably once a quarter. Consider meeting with your tax preparer before the end of the year, not just at tax time. You should be meeting with your estate planning attorney at least once every three years—and certainly when you hit the key life cycle events above. Every time you miss a meeting, you increase the chance of your estate plan failing in one way or another.

Better yet, assemble the three-person dream team of your lawyer, financial advisor, and CPA. Many clients should have these three professionals working closely together, and often. They should be so close that they have each other's cell phone numbers.

Unfortunately, most estate planning attorneys do not understand this "relationship requirement." Truly, 80 percent of attorneys will write up your plan and say goodbye forever, with no follow-up. Maybe not even a Christmas card.

## CONTROLLING ONGOING "COSTS"

For many people, however, it's neither neglect nor procrastination that gets in the way of planning and reviews. It's the fear of attorney fees. People in their thirties may not believe they have the time and money to hire an attorney for an estate plan—vital as that plan may be. People in their fifties may resent getting charged every time they call their attorney for advice. People in their seventies and eighties need their attorneys most, but may be living on fixed incomes with few dollars available for legal help.

Attorneys who actually recognize the need for a long-term maintenance plan will likely approach the problem in one of three ways:

1. Your attorney may charge an annual maintenance fee, which includes ongoing contact and education, along with regular reviews and rewrites whenever needed. The annual fee includes all necessary services.
2. Your attorney may stay in touch and provide education without a fee, be available for free calls, advice, and regular reviews—but charge a fee for rewrites.
3. Your attorney may send you newsletters and invite you to seminars, but will charge you on an hourly basis every time you call or need any services at all.

Our firm goes with option two. We know that clients don't necessarily need us every year. But we like to tell them, "Look, if you have a question, call us, no charge." We know that one day, they will be sitting at a bank having a hard time opening an account in the name of their trust. Why? Because the clerk across the desk is a fool with no education, earning $12 an hour.

At that moment, we want our client to pick up the phone, so we can tell them the magic words which will get the clerk to do his job.

Clients often call with more serious questions. "My son is getting married next week, but I'm not sure the marriage is going to last. Does my estate protect his inheritance if he were to get divorced?"

If clients had to pay us for calls and once-every-three-year reviews, the contacts might not happen. And as a result, their estate plans might not succeed. I discuss attorney business models more fully in the Introduction. But let me just say that in the best models, the law firm succeeds when the client succeeds.

Beyond the business model, I do recommend a larger firm with a support staff and a succession plan for its attorneys, so that your attorney isn't flying solo, does not retire at the same time as you, or disappear and leave you out in the cold.

One tell: solo attorneys get sued more often because they mess up more often. How do I know this? The malpractice insurance that any reputable lawyer should have is about three times as expensive for a solo attorney than it is per attorney when attorneys work together in a firm.

## STAYING EDUCATED

Beyond engaging professional help on a regular basis, you need some basic education, so you can spot the inevitable changes. You need to at least "know what you don't know" about your estate plan, your taxes, and your investments.

By reading this book, you are making a good start. Store this book in the drawer with your estate plan, and pull them both out whenever something important happens in your life. Reread the relevant sections before your three-year reviews. Use the estate planning issues' checklist until this book becomes dog-eared.

Both financial planning and estate planning firms may provide ongoing education for their clients. Go to those seminars. Read their newsletters.

# PROCRASTINATING

If you have read any part of this book, you will not be surprised when I name "procrastination" as the number one mistake made in estate planning. About 60 percent of Americans end up making an estate plan of some kind. That means 40 percent never do anything at all. Of those who make a plan, I'd say 80 percent don't keep them properly updated.

Why do we procrastinate about something so important?

Maybe we do not want to think about death and illness. Maybe we think the legal and financial stuff is too complicated for us. Maybe we don't think we should care what happens to our heirs when we die.

I know that many people suffer from "analysis paralysis." They'll say, "I want to give this serious study before I embark on a plan." But their study goes on forever.

Then again, most people just hate paperwork. My uncle, a very successful business person and a veteran of the Marine Corps, is one of my heroes. He likes to say that if he has ten tasks to do, and there's one he really doesn't like, he does that one first. In this final chapter, let me call on you to do *this one first*. Find an attorney. Make your estate plan. Get it done now.

## TRAGIC PROCRASTINATION

Throughout this book I have given many examples of people who did not plan, with awful results. As we close, let me offer just one more example: a simple tale of tragic procrastination.

We once had a wealthy businesswoman as a client. She had a large estate and needed a complex plan with multiple trusts. She knew she was dying of cancer, and she wanted to get everything just right. We worked for a long time on her plan, then called her in to sign. She was too busy to come over. We sent the papers to her office. We bugged her for weeks.

At last, she passed away, and her son came in with her pile of documents.

"At least Mom did this whole estate plan before she died," he said.

We pulled out the papers and went through them one by one. Not one had a signature. All the documents were useless.

I cannot tell you how many people bring us an unsigned living trust created by their parents. You may find it hard to believe that anyone would procrastinate to that degree, but you would be wrong. Unsigned trusts are a very common and always tragic reality of my profession.

In fact, I'm pretty sure that someone reading these words right now is thinking, "Oh, yeah, that's me. I didn't sign my trust."

## INACTION IS A KIND OF ACTION

Your estate plan is your legacy. This legacy will be different for everyone. Money may be central to your legacy, and it may not. Either way, you have the opportunity to leave a legacy of joy and harmony—or of frustration, anger, and discord.

Procrastination does not actually represent *indecision*. It represents a *bad decision*. It means you are letting unknown parties, unknown laws, and unknown processes take control of your life. For you and your heirs, this will often include courts, predators, and arguments.

On a philosophical level, you might even say that there's *really no such thing as inaction*. By doing nothing, you set in motion a series of events. It's just a very different series of events than if you did the right thing.

Age matters in this equation, because the risk of inaction increases with every day that passes. Do not wait until your mental faculties slow. Do not wait until your kids are begging you to act. Do not wait until they come to you and say, "Mom, Dad, you're killing us because you won't do this. You're making our lives harder."

**GETTING STARTED**

Yes, estate planning is complicated. As you now understand, it's too complicated to do yourself. But if you look around, you will find a few honest, highly trained people who do this every single day—dedicated people who honestly want to help other people get this right. Their motivation is sometimes personal. They've been through some terrible situations in their own families, and they want to make sure you don't make the same mistakes. It's become their passion.

Where to start? Read the section in the Introduction about

choosing a good attorney (see Introduction). Then pick up the phone and make an appointment.

Need some names? You can ask your friends and families for referrals. But here's a tip if you have no one to ask. Earlier I mentioned an organization called WealthCounsel. It's a national network of attorneys, and someone in that network will probably have an office within driving distance of where you live.

I mention this organization because the members have invested significant time, resources, and training to become members. As of this writing, it's the only organization of its kind with any significance. I'm not endorsing WealthCounsel or any of its members, but it's a good place to start. See www.wealthcounsel.com.

## DID I DO MY JOB?

If I did my job with this book, you now have a pretty solid idea of what you don't know about estate planning. If you go back to that pie chart in the Introduction, I'm hoping the "don't know what you don't know" slice has been reduced at least a bit.

If you feel more confident about walking into a firm of estate attorneys and making sure they do their job, that's a bonus.

If you feel empowered to make decisions, make them now, and keep on making them, then I will have truly fulfilled my mission.

Let us all take control of our lives in the here and now.

Let us all leave beautiful legacies.

# PREPARING FOR YOUR ESTATE PLANNING MEETING

---

Meeting with an estate attorney can be more than a tad stressful. Deep, complicated emotions may be unearthed—including plenty of issues you may never have considered. Like who, exactly, would you want looking after your minor children if you and your spouse were hit by a truck? Or what about that son-in-law who really likes to gamble: What exactly would happen if your daughter suddenly inherited a million dollar investment fund?

A good estate attorney will dig deep to discover not just problems, but *opportunities* you never considered, as well. That might include things like Roth IRA conversions or tax-advantaged charitable trusts.

In order to enable your attorney to play their proper role, you should come prepared with all the information, and at least some of the decisions they're going to need from you. No getting around it—estate planning requires *lots* of information and tough decisions.

*Both you and your attorney will save huge amounts of time (and potentially, money) if you assemble what you can in advance.*

Here's a checklist of the items and basic decisions any good attorney will request from you. If they don't ask for all this stuff, believe me, they're not doing their job.

1.  Any previous estate planning documents you have signed.
2.  A written list of questions you have up front about the process or the issues you know you will face.
3.  Full immediate family information, including full names, ages, and contact information. Make sure to include not just present, but former spouses, children, grandchildren, and stepchildren. Your attorney will need all these full names and contacts regardless of whether you intend to include them in your will or trust.
4.  Any pre-nuptial or other marital agreements.
5.  Any other agreements with family members, written or verbal.
6.  Your overall, up-to-date financial statement, if one

exists, along with the following bank and investment information. Your attorney is more interested in titling and account data from the below, but if you share the value amounts, they may be able to provide a more savvy estate plan for you:

A. Recent statements from your bank.

B. Recent statements from your investment firms. Also stock certificates, bonds, treasury notes and the like.

C. Recent statements from retirement account institutions including beneficiary information like PODs. This will include traditional IRAs, Roth IRAs, 401(k)s, 403(b)s, 457s, TSPs, any inherited retirement accounts, and any existing or anticipated pension information.

7. The deeds to your house and any other real properties you own or have any interest in, along with full property addresses, ownership interest type (sole, tenants-in-common, joint, etc.), an approximate market value, and any outstanding mortgage balances.

8. Any annuity statements and contracts, including exact beneficiary information.

9. Full information on any life insurance policies of any kind, including exact beneficiary information.

10. Contact information for any attorneys, CPAs, financial advisors, or insurance agents you work with.

11. Contact information for your primary care physician or any medical specialists you see regularly.

12. Contact information for any key clergy in your life.

13. Contact information for any charities you would like to support in your estate plan.
14. Full names and contact information on anyone else who may be involved in your estate plan in any way: such as guardians, healthcare agents, possible beneficiaries, possible fiduciary agents, and the like.
15. Any knowledge you have of anticipated inheritances of your own.
16. Information about any business interests you may have, including the full company address, etc.
17. Full names and contact information on any current business partners.
18. A list of any major personal property, like cars, boats, furniture, jewelry, valuable art—as well as ownership status.
19. Annuity contracts and statements.
20. Any debts you owe, or receivables you are legally entitled to collect.
21. Any present or future interest you have as a beneficiary or trustee in any kind of trust. This includes...
22. Any custodial accounts where you have authority over a trust or account, say, for your children or another relative.
23. Any trusts you have established or trusts created by others where you have a general power of attorney.
24. Any tax shelters or tax-deferred accounts, such as a real estate limited partnership, HSAs, FSAs, etc.
25. Any substantial monetary or property gifts you have made in the past (anything over $16,000).

26. Any recent transfers of properties or life insurance policies (within the last 3 years).

Along with all that information, it's well to begin sketching out some key decisions before your meeting with an attorney. They will help you work through these questions, but it's best to at least pencil in some answers before your meeting.

1. How would you like to divide up your assets after you pass away?
2. Is there anyone you would not like to inherit any of your property?
3. Are there specific items you'd like to go to specific people?
4. Would you like to leave a bequest to a charity, a religious institution, a university, or other worthy cause?
5. Who seems like the best person to act as executor of your will and/or trustee of your living trust, after you pass away? What two alternates to that person would make sense, in what order?
6. If you have minor children, who would you like to appoint as their physical guardian if necessary? And what two alternates?
7. It might make sense to have a different guardian for your minor children's assets and finances. If so, who would be best in that role, and what two alternates, in what order?

8. Who would you like to give a Durable Power of Attorney to manage your finances and affairs if you were incapacitated, but alive? And what two alternates, in what order?

9. Who do you trust to make healthcare decisions for you if you are incapacitated? (May or may not be the same as the above) And what two alternates, in what order?

10. Have you thought about instructions you would like to give to your healthcare agent or doctors if you were close to death? Would you want extraordinary measures like intubation to keep you alive if there appeared to be no hope?

11. Do you have specific instructions you would like to give about your funeral arrangements?

12. Would you want to donate your organs or body to science?

Tough questions? You bet. Necessary questions for you to answer? Without a doubt.

All the best,
Jim

# THE ESTATE PLANNING ISSUES CHECKLIST

———

# THE ESTATE PLANNING ISSUES CHECKLIST

| Reviewed | Issues Checklist | Reference | Notes |
|---|---|---|---|
| | **Choosing an Estate Planning Attorney** | Introduction | |
| | Does the firm specialize in estate planning? | Introduction | |
| | What is their fee structure? Packages or flat fees are best; avoid pure hourly charges. | Introduction | |
| | Do they offer free follow-up for changes? | Introduction | |
| | Does your state have a legal certification program for estate planning? | Introduction | |
| | Are the attorneys at the firm certified specialists in estate planning? | Introduction | |
| | Does the firm have a detailed process for creating a custom estate plan? | Introduction | |
| | Does the firm offer long-term care planning? | Introduction | |
| | Does the attorney belong to professional associations? | Introduction | |
| | **House and Properties** | Mistake #8 | |
| | Are you passing on a property that might create a liability for an heir? | Mistake #8 | |
| | Is your house included in your living trust? | Mistake #8 | |
| | Did you return your house to the living trust after refinancing? | Mistake #8 | |
| | **Land** | Mistake #4 | |
| | Consider a charitable trust to reduce property taxes and estate value for tax savings. | Mistake #4 | |
| | **Businesses** | Mistake #8 | |
| | Are you passing on a business that might create a liability for an heir? | Mistake #8 | |
| | Are powers of attorney established for business decisions in case of your incapacity or death? | Mistake #8 | |
| | **Problem Heirs** | Mistake #7 | |
| | Do you have any potentially irresponsible heirs? Consider a trust to create a monthly stipend instead of a one-time behest. | Mistake #7 | |
| | Should you consider having a trust protector? | Mistake #7 | |

| Reviewed | Issues Checklist | Reference | Notes |
|---|---|---|---|
| | **Planning for Changes and Updates** | Mistake #2 | |
| | When children arrive | Mistake #2 | |
| | At age eighteen, powers of attorney for healthcare and other documents | Mistake #2 | |
| | Age fifty-five review | Mistake #2 | |
| | Age sixty review | Mistake #2 | |
| | Age sixty-five review | Mistake #2 | |
| | Age seventy review | Mistake #2 | |
| | Age seventy-five review | Mistake #2 | |
| | Age eighty and up review | Mistake #2 | |
| | **IRAs** | Mistake #5 | |
| | Understand RMDs starting at age seventy-two | Mistake #5 | |
| | Make sure heirs do not withdraw IRAs too soon; stretch out IRA as long as possible | Mistake #5 | |
| | Understand the IRA tables | Mistake #5 | |
| | Keep your IRA outside of your living trust | Mistake #5 | |
| | Consider creating an IRA Legacy Trust | Mistake #5 | |
| | **401(k)s** | Mistake #5 | |
| | **PODs and TODs** | Mistake #3 | |
| | **Core Documents Signed** | Introduction | |
| | Living trust | Introduction | |
| | Advance healthcare directive (power of attorney for healthcare) | Mistake #8 | |
| | Durable power of attorney for property | Mistake #8 | |
| | Pour-over will | Mistake #8 | |
| | HIPAA authorization | Mistake #8 | |
| | **Life Insurance Complexities** | Mistake #5 | |
| | Protect life insurance from predators | Mistake #5 | |
| | Make sure heirs know about life insurance policies | Mistake #5 | |
| | **Annuities** | Mistake #5 | |
| | Annuities generally outside of trusts, controlled by beneficiaries | Mistake #5 | |

| Reviewed | Issues Checklist | Reference | Notes |
|---|---|---|---|
| | **Minor Children** | Mistake #10 | |
| | Review guardianship nomination. | Introduction | |
| | Nominate a guardian if both parents die or become incapacitated. | Introduction | |
| | Nominate successor guardians if the primary guardian is unable to serve. | Introduction | |
| | Should you consider having a trust protector? | Mistake #7 | |
| | **Divorce: Protecting Against Divorce of Heirs** | Mistake #6 | |
| | **Divorce: Protecting Against Your Own Divorce** | Mistake #6 | |
| | **Creditors: Protecting Heirs Against Creditors and Predators** | Mistake #6 | |
| | **Planning for Your Own Possible Disability or Incapacity** | Mistake #8 | |
| | Study Mistake #8 in detail. | Mistake #8 | |
| | Establish powers of attorney for healthcare issues. | Mistake #8 | |
| | Establish powers of attorney for property. | Mistake #8 | |
| | Create or update your HIPAA authorization. | Mistake #8 | |
| | **Dependents Who Are Disabled or Incapacitated** | Mistake #7 | |
| | **Spousal Inheritance** | Mistake #4 | |
| | Check with an attorney if you have an existing A-B trust; it may be obsolete. | Mistake #4 | |
| | Trusts can be structured to protect against "high-maintenance spouses" of beneficiaries. | Mistake #6 | |
| | **State-Specific Issues** | Mistake #4 | |
| | Understand unusual state issues such as "decoupled states" with their own inheritance taxes. | Mistake #4 | |
| | **Charity and Charitable Tax Reduction** | Mistake #4 | |
| | Consider a charitable trust. | Mistake #4 | |
| | Consider a charitable remainder annuity trust. | Mistake #4 | |
| | Consider a charitable gift annuity. | Mistake #4 | |

# ABOUT THE AUTHOR

———

**JAMES L. CUNNINGHAM, JR.** has been an attorney for more than two decades in the areas of estate planning, probate, trust administration, elder law, disability/special needs planning, and much more. He is one of the few attorneys certified by the State Bar of California as a Specialist in Estate Planning, Trust, and Probate Law. As founder of CunninghamLegal, he oversees twelve offices, along with a team of attorneys and professionals focused entirely on estate issues. James is a California native, a devoted husband, and the father of three children. You can learn more about his work at cunninghamlegal.com.